UNAPOLOGETICALLY CONFIDENT

THE LITTLE
BLACK BOOK
OF
MODELING

Beginner & Intermediate Career Guide

"DON'T LOOK TO THE LEFT OR RIGHT. STAY FOCUSED".

By
DAMIA GORDON

Published by Parker & Co., LLC

P.O. Box 50040

Richmond, VA 23250

Copyright © 2022

All Rights Reserved. Violators will be prosecuted by local, state, and federal law.

No part of this publication may be reproduced, stored in any retrieval system, or transmitted in any form or by any means, including photocopying, recording, or any other way without the written permission of the author.

We greatly appreciate you for buying an authorized copy of this book and for complying with the copyright laws by not reproducing, scanning, or distributing any part of this book in any form without permission. You are supporting the hard work of authors by doing so.

ISBN: (paperback): 979-8-432791-66-5
ISBN: (hardback): 978-1-952733-49-9
ISBN: (ebook): 978-1-952733-51-2

Dedication

I would like to dedicate my book to God, Natasha McCrea, Audrey Hinds, Michelle R. Hannah, Marshaé Bray, Katrina Graham, Eli Hicks, Ron Harrison, my daughter Yasmine Fortson, my parents, my brother, and all my supporters because without them, I would've never gotten this far to write this book.

Disclaimer

This book doesn't guarantee success. When you put in the work, you will see the results you apply. This book is designed to guide, encourage, and educate and enhance you in the modeling industry, where your growth is dependent on your dedication, resources, and consistency.

Table of Contents

Introduction: My Story 1

Session 1: So You Want to Model?

Quick Model Steps 7

Chapter 1: How to Become a Model 8

Chapter 2: Branding & Investing in Yourself 10

    Comp Card 10

    Headshots 13

    Portfolio 15

    Modeling Business Cards 15

    Model Résumé 16

    Model Stats 16

    Modeling Email Address Professionalism 17

    Video Content 17

    YouTube Channel 18

    Instagram Reels 18

    Mentorship 19

    Model Bootcamp 19

    Website 20

Chapter 3: Haters Do Exist 21

    Protect Yourself & Brand 21

    Health Insurance 23

Session 2: Slay, Honey, Slay

Chapter 4: Stay Ready 27
- What to Pack for Model Calls/Fashion Shows 27
- Model Casting Calls 27
- Fashion Shows.. 29

Chapter 5: Practice & Perfect Your Skill 33
- Posing 33
- Walking.. 34
- How Often Should You Practice?... 35

Chapter 6: I Am the Living Hanger 36
- Modeling Fashion Styles... 36
- Lifestyle 37
- Fashion/Editorial 38
- Fitness Models 39
- Swimsuit & Lingerie Models 40
- Commercial Models 41
- Runway Models 42
- Print Models... 43
- Child Models.. 44
- Teen Models... 44
- Parts Models.. 44
- Glamour Models.. 44
- Fit Models... 44
- Promotional Models 45
- Plus Size/Petite Models... 45

Chapter 7: Modeling Tips to Slay the Runway...............................47

Chapter 8: Grab Your Passport, Honey! 50

Chapter 9: Brand Ambassador...58

Page | v

Session 3: Speaking My Self-Care Language

Chapter 10: Your Self-Care Royalty 62

Chapter 11: Self-Development & Evaluation 67
    Strengths 67
    Weaknesses 68
    Opportunities 68
    Threats 69

Chapter 12: Mindset: The Power of the Mind 70

Chapter 13: Trusting Yourself 73
    Trust Starts Within 73
    The 5 C's to Live By 74

Session 4: Girl, I Got the TEA

Chapter 14: Resolution to the Lies & Scams 80
    What the Industry Is Not Telling You 80
    Stay in Safety Mode 85

Chapter 15: Won't Stop, Can't Stop Learning 87

Chapter 16: Modeling Etiquette: Your Reputation Precedes You ... 89

Chapter 17: Modeling Industry Standards 92
    Do Age, Height, Weight, or Race Matter in This Industry? 92
    If I Have a Disability, Can I Still Be a Model? 93

Session 5: Identity Check

Chapter 18: Don't Chase the Hype; Chase the Dream 95

Chapter 19: Social Media Elevation 96
    Instagram Tips for Your Modeling Page 96

Photo Quality vs. Quantity.. 98

Chapter 20: Facing Rejection, My Closest Enemy 100

Chapter 21: Don't Stand in the Way of Your Dreams 102

Session 6: Cash Me on the Go, Honey

Chapter 22: Model on the Go 105
   Keep Track & Follow-up 105
   Track Your Journey! 107

Chapter 23: Budgeting Expenses & Closure....................................114

Session 7: Girl, Cross That Finish Line

Chapter 24: Choosing an Agency 118
   What is a Modeling Agency? 118
   Dive into the Agency Details 118

Chapter 25: Did I Just Hit a Plateau? 120

Chapter 26: Opportunities Galore 121

Chapter 27: You Made It! 125

Advanced Tactics... 127
   Modeling Consultant Services 127
   Modeling Glossary 127

Reference websites... 131
   Modeling Picture Album.. 132

Introduction

My Story

Everyone has a story of how and why they became who they are. We struggle to decide whether we want to share it, what parts to expose, what parts to keep a secret, and whether we tell it all. Well, I'm a part of everyone, and I have a story, too. It's not that pretty, but it's very real, so get ready to get uncomfortable.

Here goes.

I never saw myself as a model because I always looked at my past life experiences, and what society or the modeling /entertainment industry considered a "model." Society sets such high standards on what qualifies as beautiful. Growing up, while in school and in one of my past relationships, I was told I was fat, ugly, had a big nose, and was too short. I used to look at America's Next Top Model and say, "Wow, I would love to model one day, but I'm nothing compared to those models." After a while, I believed all the negative thoughts people spoke into my spirit. They played over and over in my subconscious, and I began to sabotage myself.

In one of my past relationships, I tried to please my boyfriend by trying to become the woman he's always wanted. As a result of being unable to fulfill his desires, I went through a state of depression and lost 20 pounds in a week in a half because I stopped living life. I thought maybe if I was skinnier, he would love me more. Then at one point, I ended up in the hospital lying in bed with tubes in my nose, and IVs in my arm due to dehydration, the doctor said. I was so stressed, and I didn't like who I had become. In other areas of my life, I loss so much, like my house, my job, close friends, mentally abused, and among other things. By this time, I had a daughter as well, and I didn't want her to see my struggles but wanted to do everything I could to allow her to feel loved and secure. I hid a lot of things from her because it wasn't her stress to carry. A child deserves to live and be a child. Deep inside, I felt like there was no hope and that no one loved me. I stopped talking, smiling, and being me. My last solution was to try to commit suicide because I felt life wasn't worth living.

Once I became free of the toxic relationships and mental negativity that set me back, God gave me clarity in realizing there is purpose to my life. What people said were my flaws, I made them my strength. I decided to speak words of affirmation into my life, design the life I wanted as my coach always told me, and overcame my fear by volunteering to model in my first fashion show for Black Business Women Rock in November 2018, which was a large networking event. I have to say, negative thoughts did cross my mind when I saw all the other models, how tall and slim they were. I told myself, "I may be the shortest and curviest model out of all of them, but I'm going to bring it." Walking the runway for the first time left me with a sense of confidence and boldness. I finally found something I passionately enjoyed doing!!! Since modeling in that fashion show, I have built my confidence and self-worth, feeling like every "no" gets me closer to a "yes." I am now highly recommended. My official modeling journey took off

MY STORY

in April 2019. In my first nine months of modeling in 2019, I've been booked for fashion shows, photoshoots, and brand ambassador opportunities almost every weekend—and during the week. I am a brand ambassador for several clothing lines and the face of a beauty brand, and I have been a modeling coach for a fashion show. Here is a synopsis of some of my accomplishments:

- Modeled in 50+ fashion shows
- Became brand ambassador for 20+ brands
- Completed numerous photoshoots
- Published in multiple magazines
- Featured in a movie, "A Holiday Chance," which came out in theaters November 2021
- Will be featured in two more upcoming movies in 2022
- Crowned Ms. California US Nation
- Crowned Ms. Global Noble
- Runway model for New York Fashion Week 2022
- My daughter and I named model finalist for Cynthia Bailey's "The Bailey Agency" (from Real Housewives of Atlanta), categories for plus-size model and teen model, 3 times in a row
- Listed on countless websites as a model
- Met the executive producers of "Dancing with the Stars" along with countless celebrities while in a fashion show

- Met the Queen of Liberia as a trophy model for THE HAPA AWARDS
- Started my own modeling consultant business, Confident Curvess, LLC, to mentor models looking to get into the industry

I never imagined this could happen to me!!! I'm so grateful!!!

I am truly blessed by every opportunity God has given me and will continue to give me. I am a single mom, but it doesn't stop me from being confident, fierce, sassy, classy, and expressing my personality. Modeling is so much fun!! Every step that I take while on the runway or at a photoshoot gives me the motivation to be the sassy classy model I've always dreamed of. I've inspired my daughter to model, and she too modeled at one point, but she is currently focused on her college education, majoring in computer science!!!

I've decided to go after my success! It's not easy, but success looks like this for me: first of all, trusting God; then tests, trials, networking, supporting/inspiring others, staying consistent, believing in myself, failing at times, conquering my fears, speaking words of affirmation, staying focused on my vision, and knowing there is purpose in helping others to fulfill their dreams. Some seasons in my life are better than others, but no matter the season or flaws, I walk confident in my spirit, and work on my subconscious. As I reach higher levels of success, I continue to stay humble, take those with me that want to go, always be teachable, and know NOTHING is impossible no matter my situation. When I'm down, I fight back because I know I can get back up again. I am a sophisticated BOSS woman that is beautiful,

MY STORY

educated, gifted, a talented cook and a runway model that commands the room with class and a twist of sass.

My goal is to inspire and motivate everyone that no matter what people say you can't do, you can do it. Even with the flaws you think you have, know that you are still valuable, unique, and can do anything that you believe you can do!

Session 1

SO YOU WANT TO MODEL?

Quick Model Steps

- Work on your CONFIDENCE!!!!
- Study the industry.
- Purchase modeling items.
- Practice walking and posing.
- Find clothes to wear that will look great on camera and present you well.
- Find a photographer to set up 2-3 photoshoot sessions.
- Attend photoshoot appointments. (Bring at least two different looks.)
- Get a Comp Card.
- Create an Instagram page and post your first photo.
- Attend some fashion shows to become familiar with what you should expect.
- Search for model casting calls, fashion shows, other opportunities, or sign up with an agency.
- Manage your calendar and follow-up.
- Be consistent, persistent, and focused.
- Establish a budget for modeling.
- Always invest in yourself.
- NEVER GIVE UP!!

1

How to Become a Model

Where should I go? Who should I talk to? Where do I start? Do I have what it takes to be a model? Am I the right height? How can I get paid to be a model? The questions and thoughts that plague your mind are very normal and valid. Take a deep breath. Breathe in and out. Now, let's talk about it.

There are several ways you can go about it, but you want to work smarter and not harder. First things first before I get into the logistics. Work on your confidence. Your confidence is everything. Identify the areas in your life that cause you to lack in your confidence.

One way you can go about it is being a freelance model by learning the educational side of modeling. Watch tons of modeling YouTube videos (e.g., how to pose, modeling tips, starting a modeling career, tricks to looking good in photos as a model, what modeling agencies look for, building a portfolio as a model, etc.), watch modeling TV shows to pick up some techniques, and practice while you learn. This option can be a bit draining and can take a lot longer to arrive at your destination. This option also includes the delay in getting continuous paid gigs, signing large paid contracts to be a brand ambassador with reputable companies, or other obstacles along the way. Now, I will say as a freelance model, there are still great benefits and rewards, the further you grow in your journey. One of the biggest benefits is your freedom to control your career. All the money you negotiate as a model, you get to keep--every dime. #momoney #momoney #momoney

The second way is hiring a modeling runway coach and attending bootcamps.

The third way is signing with a modeling agency. Out of all these options, you still must put in the work to get the results you are looking for. Last, think globally. You don't have to settle to be a model in just one state. You can travel the world and be an international runway model. Becoming a model is not always about how beautiful you are. It's about the uniqueness of who you are. Make sure you stand out for all the right reasons. Now put on your big girl panties, buckle your seatbelt, and get ready for the time of your life. Great things are getting ready to happen, so LET'S GO!!!!

2

Branding & Investing in Yourself

It's important that anything you desire to do, you invest in yourself to be better than who you are today. When I first started off in the industry, I had no clue what I was doing or what I needed. As I received more opportunities for fashion shows, photoshoots, and more, I learned quickly I was missing key components I needed to advance in the modeling industry. As an aspiring model in the beginning stages, I learned there are key areas you benefit from when investing in yourself.

Comp Card

What is it? A Comp Card is a common marketing tool to help promote you. It can also be your business card. It is typically used in the modeling and entertainment industry to showcase you in different styles.

Comp card complete: Yes/No _____ How Many _____

BRANDING & INVESTING IN YOURSELF

When do you use Comp Cards? Comp Cards are sometimes requested at model calls, photoshoots, acting auditions, etc.

What should the Comp Card consist of? Name, email address, contact #, social media handler, measurements (height, bust, hips, waist, shoe size, eyes & hair color), and 3-5 professional pictures of different styles. Memorize your measurements.

Additional measurements? Yes, sometimes additional measurements are requested by the designer, especially if the designer is designing a custom outfit. Some of the additional measurements include neck, under bust, shoulder, shoulder to waist (front/back), arm length, bicep, back width, hip height, thigh, leg length, waist to floor, and neck to floor.

MODEL STANDARD MEASUREMENTS

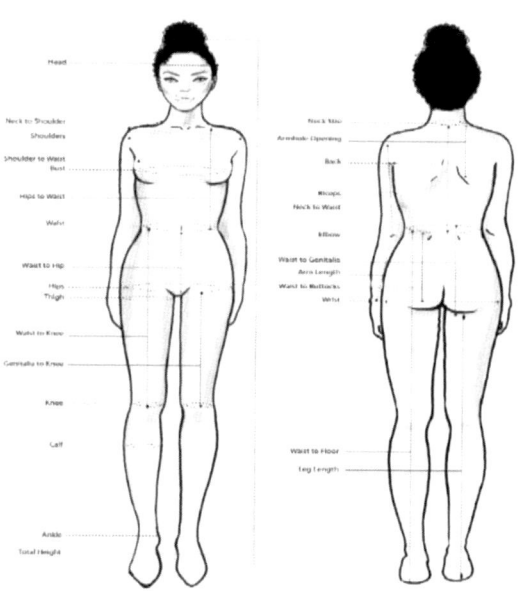

Bust	33"
Waist	26"
Hip	36"
Head	23"
Neck Size	15"
Shoulders	16"
Shoulder to Waist	12.7"
Neck to Shoulder	4.9"
Hips to Waist	10.7"
Neck to Waist	16"
Armhole Opening	8.6"
Arm Length	24"
Bicep	10.6"
Elbow	8.6"
Wrist	6.29"
Waist to Knee	23.4"
Waist to Hip	7.8"
Waist to Floor	40.9"
Waist to Buttocks	11"
Thigh	20.5"
Knee	13.6"
Calf	13.8"
Leg Length	33"
Ankle	9.3"
Genitalia to Knee	13"
Waist to Genitalia	7"
Back	13.5"
Total Height	5'9"

MODELING BEGINNERS GUIDE

MODEL STANDARD MEASUREMENTS
LABEL YOUR MEASUREMENTS

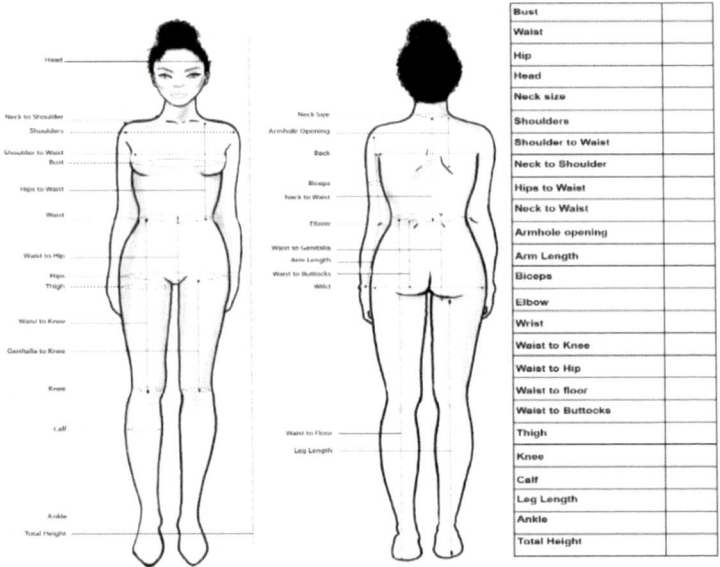

Average cost of Comp Cards. Price may vary depending on quantity: $35-$185. Price subject to change due to price fluctuation and market value.

How many should I have available? 25-50. Update every 6 months or after a year.

How do I get a Comp Card? Utilize my services, create the Comp Card yourself, inquire from a photographer, or have an agency to create one for you. If you decide to create your own Comp Card, I would recommend using zazzle.com, vistaprint.com, or Etsy.com

BRANDING & INVESTING IN YOURSELF

Example of Comp Card below

Headshots

What is a headshot? A headshot is a model's business card or Comp Card. Unlike a Comp Card, the headshot focuses more on the person. It showcases the model's natural looks. The headshot should consist of one professional picture, very little to no makeup. It is not glamour time, so don't look like you are going over the top. It should be very simple, showcasing your natural beauty. The client needs to see what you look like with very too little to no makeup. Here are some tips to keep in mind when taking a professional picture for a headshot. Avoid busy patterns and stripes; they're distractions. If you want to look slimmer in your pictures, choose outfits that are more fitting to your shape and tactful. Your sleeves shouldn't look like you are getting ready to take off in the winter. They should be flattering. Make sure to have a variety of necklines to show different looks. Jewelry should be very simple and not overpowering. Bring colors that go well with your skin.

Headshot Example

Photographer – Stephanie Oliver, Instagram @believeit.2inspire

Personality? Everyone has a personality. Now is not the time to hide yours. Clients love to see what type of personality you have on camera. Sometimes it can make or break you.

Portfolio

What is it? According to adorama.com, your portfolio is your résumé. It is a tool to help you make a good impression and showcase what you can do. This is a good selling point to submit to modeling agencies.

How do I build my portfolio? You can use mixbook.com, inquire from a photographer, or speak with an agency.

What do a portfolio consist of? For professional models, a portfolio consists of 20 pictures, different modeling styles, facial expressions, poses, and various clients you've worked with. Most of all, your portfolio should showcase your talent as a model (e.g., professional picture of you playing your guitar).

Modeling Business Cards

What is it? Modeling business cards are similar to your Comp Card; however, they are smaller. It can be in the form of hard copy or digital.

What Information should it consist of? It consists of an extraordinary picture of you, your first and last names, phone number, email address, Instagram handle, and website, if created professionally. I recommend you google examples as a point of reference.

How can I create my business cards? I recommend zazzle.com or vistaprint.com.

How many to have available? 25-50, or create a QR Code for others to scan to pull up your information digitally.

Average cost? $30 and up, depending on quantity, subject to change due to price fluctuation and market value.

Model Résumé

What is a model résumé? Your modeling résumé showcases who you are and what you've accomplished in the modeling industry, such as editorial shoots, commercials, TV shows, fashion shows you were in, print work, etc. Your résumé is also similar to how you sell yourself to employers when applying for a job. It also helps agencies to determine whether they would like to use your services in various areas of the modeling industry.

How do I create a modeling résumé? You can use an online template and google "Runway Model Resume Sample." You can also consult with an agency to assist you.

Model Stats

What is it? Model stats is a pay rate scale often used to pay models.

How to determine your rate? Determine your rate based on your level of experience and exposure.

Average Rates? $50-$100 per hour or higher depending on your contract/agreement. Subject to change due to price fluctuation and market value.

When to request pay? When you've developed enough experience and exposure. DO NOT wait years to get paid. Give yourself a time limit of when you will no longer accept volunteer opportunities. Otherwise, you will always work for free. You will know when the time is right.

What date did you decide you will no longer be free?

_____

Now stick to it, and believe paid opportunities will come your way. Don't give up!

Modeling Email Address Professionalism

Should I have a separate email address for modeling? Yes. this will help you to keep track and be more organized on your modeling journey.

What email address did you decide to go with?

_____

Don't use slang or profanity in your email address. Be professional in how you represent yourself. Use common sense, girl!

Video Content

Why choose video content? Investing in professional video content will definitely set you apart from most models. It can capture your modeling journey and give them insight into your story and who you are. **Contacts available upon request.**

YouTube Channel

Should I start a YouTube channel? Yes!! Having a YouTube channel allows your audience to follow your journey on a personal level. You can also share your experiences, good or bad, about the industry, and increase your social media followers as well. People love authenticity, so show them who you are.

How do I start a YouTube channel? Google "How to start a YouTube channel." It's that simple.

Can I get paid? Yes! You can earn and learn at the same time. This would be a great source for another stream of income.

What's your YouTube channel name?

_____

Did you post your YouTube video? If so, when?

_____

Instagram ReelsPassive Income: Instagram Reels Capitalization

Technology is constantly changing, so why not capitalize on the *now* of your brand, so you can enjoy and reap the blessings of your future? One of the hottest attractive upcoming passive income options are Instagram Reels!

What are Instagram Reels? Instagram Reels are short 30-60 second creative videos you can post on Instagram that will take your brand to a whole new level.

What are the benefits of creating Reels on Instagram? Your videos will come to life in a whole new way. When you create your Reels on Instagram, you have the possibility of going viral, increasing your followers, gaining great business exposure, and receiving more opportunities. I can attest, I #love creating my Reels on Instagram. I am gaining so many new followers that some of my Reels on Instagram have gone viral, and I am making great connections. Instagram also allows creators to earn up to $10,000 for posting Reels. Compensation is based on the number of views and followers for now. Technology and stipulations are subject to change, so be sure to check it out while it's hot.

How to capitalize on Instagram Reels? Check out "Creators," "Instagram for Business," and "Earn Money" through Instagram.

Mentorship

Why do I need mentorship? Mentorship is beneficial to you because it helps to guide you on your journey in knowing the do's and don'ts. Also, working with someone experienced in the industry will allow you to grow, stay focused, and be encouraged when your drive is low.

Average cost? Varies depending on the service. Average cost is $199 and up. Subject to change due to price fluctuation and market value.

Model Bootcamp

What is model bootcamp? Model bootcamp is designed to critique you on your runway walk, posing, posture, help prepare you for future modeling opportunities, commercials, casting calls, proper etiquette, integrity, ethics, and more. Model bootcamp can be a series of classes and is especially great for beginners or anyone that would like to advance their career in modeling.

Average cost? $80 and up. Subject to change due to price fluctuation and market value.

Model bootcamp Service Company _____

Cost of the service? _____

Services being rendered? _____

Website

Why is it good to have a website? Developing a modeling website/link will definitely set you apart from many models. This shows professionals you are serious about modeling. If you need assistance on setting up your website, I have the perfect contacts for you.

Average cost? Varies.

3

Haters Do Exist

Protect Yourself & Brand

Haters are always waiting to see your downfall. They thrive and gain pleasure in seeing you lose. Let me tell you how I know. My Instagram page promotes positivity, confidence, my journey as a model, supporting others, my accomplishments, fun, and excitement. If you don't believe me, go check it out at @sassyclassymodel.

Well, one day I posted a picture of me from a photoshoot in a nice black cocktail dress. My hair was laid, y'all. I looked so beautiful in that picture. People started commenting on my page, and I received so many likes. The next thing I knew, I tried to respond to some of the comments on the post to say, "Thank you." Then, all of a sudden, I received a message on Instagram saying, "We have noticed suspicious activity on your page. Please verify your identity by entering the code we just sent to the number you have on your account." I entered the code. I then received a message saying, "Thank you. For security purposes log out, log back in, and change your password." I logged out, tried to log back in, then it said, "Your account is now locked." I couldn't get back into my account, no matter how hard I tried. I tried to reach a representative, and I was still unsuccessful.

After various attempts, I had to go through Facebook to reach a representative to try to get my page back. I didn't give up! Guess how long it took me to get my page back? Two and a half months. I was so mad. The whole time I was without my page! I started a new page because I didn't want to give up, but--I have to be honest--I cried when I lost my page because that was years of content I have posted about my journey, and I had built up my followers to 2K. I felt discouraged. When Facebook/Instagram finally gave me my page back, I asked them why I couldn't access my page. They showed me the below picture & said people reported it as being inappropriate, and Instagram flagged it as "Violating Community Guidelines." They also said, "Someone probably tried to hacked your account, too." I said, "Are you KIDDING ME. ARE YOU SERIOUS???" With all the nudity, profanity, explicit language, and among other things, that picture below is "Violating Community Guidelines?!" #really #smh Make sure you put double security (two-part authentication) on all your social media platforms. The haters are coming y'all. #frfr

HATERS DO EXIST

Photographer – Kwe, Instagram @kwalityphotos
Designer – Sheba McMahon, Instagram @shebamcollection
#OMG Did I Just Trip & Fall Off the Runway?

Health Insurance

Sometimes the unexpected happens. I almost broke my thumb. Can you believe that??? Let me tell you what happened.

    I was in a fashion show looking so fly in my sexy black cocktail couture dress. We were in the middle of intermission. The announcement was made all the models can grab a plate of food in the designated area. I grabbed my plate with all the delicious food on my plate. I was so excited! I was even licking my lips because I couldn't wait to eat. I was walking to the dressing room to eat the delicious food on my plate. I sat down, and ate piece by piece, bite by bite. See as a plus size model, you can tell I don't miss even one meal. Yummy yummy in my tummy!

After finishing up, I realized that I didn't have a napkin. So I got up from my seat to walk back to the designated food area to grab a napkin. As I was walking back to the fitting room across the runway, because there was no other way to get back, my foot slipped, and I tried to catch my balance. Before I knew it, all my weight landed on my left thumb! Smh! It hurt so bad, I thought I was going to burst into tears. People were asking, "Sassy, are you okay?" I said, "Yes," thinking I was fine until we started the second half of the fashion show. The designer handed me my outfit to walk the runway. I tried to put on the pants which were part of the outfit, but I realized I couldn't use my left thumb. Someone had to help me. After the show was over, I told myself, *I probably will be in pain for about a week nothing serious.*

Well, a week went by, and I was still in pain. While at home, I reached for a glass of water and couldn't use my left thumb. After a while, I kept saying I was going to schedule an appointment with the doctor and probably need x-rays. As time went on, I noticed the bone in my left thumb was sticking out a little, and the pain never stopped. Fast forward 11 months later, and the pain was still there, and I never went to the doctor. Let me tell you how my thumb healed.

I went out with a group of ladies to a spa to get a full-body massage. The massage therapist massaged my hands and worked toward massaging my thumb. Can someone say, #painful? The massage therapist was pulling my thumb, but in the process, I didn't realize it was all for my good. After I left the massage therapist, a day later, I realized I could finally use my thumb. Yayyyy! #healed. The lesson in all this is make sure you have health insurance in place just in case you injure yourself along the way, and be sure to use it, too. Don't be like me: I had insurance, but I didn't use it when you should have.

Yasssss, Honey! You made it through session 1!!! Wooo hoooo! Congratulations! Now put on that song by Teyana Taylor: "Made It," and dance with excitement! Keep going!

Session 2

SLAY, HONEY, SLAY

4

Stay Ready

What to Pack for Model Calls/Fashion Shows

Your model items for model calls and fashion shows are so important. You can pack items in a small suitcase or duffle bag. Designers like variety so they can showcase their clothing line effectively. You can pretty much pack similar items for model calls and fashion shows. DO NOT PACK YOUR ENTIRE CLOSET.

Model Casting Calls

What is it? A model call is a visual interview audition showcasing who you are in front of the designer, client, or even casting director. Your presentation is everything. This is a great opportunity to be you by showing your personality, walk, and style.

What to wear? You should wear all black. All black items includes black tights or jeans, fitted body suit, black high heels. Do not go to the model call makeup-glamorous and lots of jewelry. Keep it simple.

Where can I purchase items? Marshalls, Ross, online stores, or any store that has the items available.

Email Follow-Up & Model Call Interest? Many of the post or advertisements will require you to submit your interest entry information via email. Be sure to submit in a timely fashion and professionally. For example, if you are submitting your information as interest in a model call, read what is required for your submission, and set email up as below:

To: designerx@gmail.com

Subject: Model Call Interest – Event Name & Date

Email Body: Hi (whom the email should be addressed to)

My name is _____. I am currently interested in being one of the models for the (event name). Here is the requested information (height, measurements, headshot or picture or modeling picture, Instagram handle or your website link).

I look forward to hearing from you soon.

Thank you,

Your Name

Contact #

If you don't hear from them by the deadline, follow-up to inquire about the status. If you still don't hear from them, MOVE ON to the next.

Quick Tip – Be sure to have a second stash of your modeling casting attire in your car, just in case you get an unexpected call. You want to always *be* ready, not *trying to get* ready.

Opportunities? Always be on the lookout for opportunities. The more you have, the more you will become comfortable and confident with modeling

Quantity? Buy two sets of each item.

Average cost of items? $80-$120. Subject to change due to price fluctuation.

Fashion Shows

What is it? Fashion Shows are events designers put on to showcase their clothing line. Fashion shows are every season.

Meet & Greet? Get to know other models, photographers, and designs. You can exchange social media and contact information. When you exchange the information, send them a quick message through Instagram, Facebook, text message, or other forms of useful communication to allow them to remember you and for you to remember them. Be sure to look out for each other when you make healthy connections.

Walking in Fashion Shows? The key to walking in any fashion show is confidence, uniqueness, and believing in yourself.

Gratitude? ALWAYS, ALWAYS thank the designer and others for allowing you to be in the show and model their clothing line. It goes a long way.

What to pack?

What to pack items in? Small suitcase or duffle bag

Tights/leggings – Black, nude, white

Jeans – Black jeans and denim

Fitted Body Suit – Black, white, nude

Nipple covers

Bras – Black or nude strapless bra, solid black bra with straps

Jewelry (optional) – Some variety of jewelry, earrings, necklace, bracelets

Makeup – Bring your makeup just in case there is no makeup artist available for the models. Sometimes it is best to come makeup-ready to get the look you desire. Know how to do your own makeup.

Hair – Designers are pretty flexible with the style of your hair. If you wear wigs, have different varieties on hand.

Nail polish – Not mandatory. However, make sure you do not have chipped nail polish. Chose the color of your choice.

High heels/shoes – Solid colors such as black and nude are common. Optional solid colors to consider include red, blue, pink, yellow, green, and maybe some animal print.

STAY READY

Deodorant – Bring deodorant just in case. Do not spray designer clothes with perfume or other products. It can damage the clothes.

Minimize armpit sweat or odor – Purchase fresh lemons. Slice in half. Squeeze lemon juice in a Ziplock bag or enough to squeeze in a bottle. Right before you put on the designer's clothes, place the lemon juice under your armpit. This helps to keep you from sweating, damaging the designer's clothes, and eliminates unnecessary odor. Hygiene is very important.

Other handy items – safety pins, hair pins, nail polish remover, fashion tape, heel cover

Please note, sometimes prior to the fashion show, designers or coordinators will send you a list of items to bring for the show. If not, make sure you ask them for those specific items you will need.

Name That Fashion Show!!! List some of the fashion shows and dates you were blessed to be a part of: e.g. "Fierce Runway/2022". Let's go!

1.
2.
3.
4.
5.
6.
7.

8. _____

9. _____

10. _____

5

Practice & Perfect Your Skill

Practice! Practice! Practice! I heard Les Brown on one of his motivational speeches say, "Many people say practice makes perfect. No. Practice makes improvement." We can never be perfect because if we are perfect, we have no room for growth. It is important to practice as much as possible to strengthen the areas needed. The more you practice, the more confidence you'll develop to become better at what you do. The goal is to ALWAYS HAVE FUN!!!

What areas should you practice as an aspiring model?

Posing

Practice posing in the mirror. DO NOT be stiff. Just relax and act normal. BE YOURSELF. Being yourself is one of the most important keys in this industry. Google different styles of posing, practice, and make them your own. Take selfies of you posing, or have someone use their phone to take pictures of you. This will help you see where you need to improve if it doesn't come naturally to you. Also, photographers love a variety of poses and angles because they give the photos more character, personality, life, and uniqueness. Practice posing 3-4 times a week for 10-20 minutes or more. The more you practice, the more natural you will be when you are at a fashion show or photoshoot.

Dates you practiced posing?

_____, _____, _____,
_____, _____, _____,
_____.

<u>Walking</u>

Practice walking different styles. For example, try walking your normal style back and forth down a hallway. Have someone videotape you with their phone so you can see what you look like. You can also go to YouTube for modeling and runway walking tips. Remember your posture is important as well. Do not walk in a fashion or model casting call with your back slouched over. Stand up straight, shoulders back, looking forward, pelvic up, stomach in, and strut yo' stuff. Say to yourself, "I am confident. I got this!" Practice walking in high heels 5 days a week for 15-30 minutes or more.

Dates you practice walking?

_____, _____, _____,
_____, _____, _____,
_____.

PRACTICE & PERFECT YOUR SKILL

How Often Should You Practice?

Practice as much as possible, but practice doing it the right way in front of a mirror! Ask yourself, "How bad do I want it? How good do I want to become?"

Dates you practiced your fierce modeling walk:

1. _____
2. _____
3. _____
4. _____
5. _____
6. _____
7. _____
8. _____
9. _____
10. _____

Are you improving? Yes or No _____

6

I Am the Living Hanger

Modeling Fashion Styles

There are so many fashion-modeling styles you should become familiar with, but some of the most common styles are below. Different styles set different moods in photos and on the runway. I recommend you do a search on the internet to have a visual of all the styles. Here is a list of the most common: fashion, editorial, fitness, print, commercial, swimsuit, lingerie, runway, parts, promotional, glamour, plus size and petite and fit model. You can also watch videos of the different types of moods that set the tone of the scene. Below are some examples of different modeling types.

I AM THE LIVING HANGER

Lifestyle

This style can be more of your casual wear but customized to your style. It captures real-life events and different moments in your life or others' lives.

Photographer – Tre Parker, Instagram @treparkerphotography
*Makeup – Katrina Graham, Instagram: @_kysses_*

Fashion/Editorial

This style is often used for high fashion/editorial models working with top fashion designers. Average height 5'9", bust 33", waist 23", hips 33" Photoshoot

Designer – Noell, Instagram @noellstore
Photographer – Tre Parker, Instagram @treparkerphotography

I AM THE LIVING HANGER

*Makeup – Katrina Graham, Instagram @_kysses_*

Fitness Models

This style is an athletic look. Models showcasing this style will wear fitness attire. This style typically showcases the fit, toned, and athletically built. Sometimes models can transition to being in athletic commercials.

MODELING BEGINNERS GUIDE

Designer – Jamall Richboy Sports, Instagram @richboysports
*Photographer – Andrea R. Holloway, @rroyal_family_*

Swimsuit & Lingerie Models

This style features models of all sizes, including curvy, plus-size models, sleepwear, summer wear, undergarments, lingerie, swimwear, and more.

Designer - W. B. E. A TheBrand Clothing, Instagram
@wbea_thebrandofcollections
Photographer - Nicole "KoKo" Dominguez, Instagram
@freshdripphotography

I AM THE LIVING HANGER

<u>Commercial Models</u>

This category is used for advertisement for products, campaigns, magazines, billboards, and more. No age, height, weight, or size is required. Advertisement is limitless for catalogs. The mood is set depending on the item being modeled.

Photographer – Paul Kiefer, Instagram @kieferstudio

MODELING BEGINNERS GUIDE

Runway Models

Models are hired to showcase a designer's clothing line on the catwalk, also known as the runway. The industry is changing in terms of height and weight requirements.

Designer – Miss Sabrak, Instagram @sabrakboutique
Photographer – Tre Parker, Instagram @treparkerphotography
Makeup – Don Hsiao, Instagram @don_hsiao

I AM THE LIVING HANGER

Print Models

Print models are models typically in magazines, billboards, campaigns, flyers, posters, websites, influencers, commercials, fun hair, and more.

Photographer – Kwe, Instagram @kwalityphotos

Child Models

Children under 12 are hired to model a designer's kid clothing line. They also may be hired for commercials, campaigns, movies, and more.

Teen Models

Adolescents between the 12-17 are hired to model a designer's clothing and to be a brand ambassador. They also may be hired for commercials, campaigns, movies, and more.

Parts Models

Parts models are models using their arms, hands, feet, and legs to showcase jewelry, shoes, nails, beauty care, and products.

Glamour Models

Models that are hired as glamour models are used to focus on their beauty and body. The beauty and body type of the model are selected based on the client's needs. Glamour models also model lingerie or are sometimes completely nude.

Fit Models

Fit models are live mannequins behind the scenes testing out designers' and clothing manufacturers' new clothes and products.

Promotional Models

Promotional models help to promote or sell company products through advertisement. They have an upbeat personality and are outgoing and knowledgeable of the product being advertised and inter with buyers.

Plus Size/Petite Models

I just have to SCREAM it loud and proud, "Plus size, curvy, and petite models MATTER TOO!" The industry is changing and starting to accept plus size, curvy, and petite queens because they deserve to be seen, too. All human beings are not all the same size. This category typically includes models starting at size 12. As a plus size petite model, I am having the time of my life being me. There is a place for you in the industry, too. There are so many opportunities available for these models just like the standard size models: print, magazines, campaigns, flyers, posters, influencers, commercials, hair industry, products, beauty, and more. Never count yourself out.

What's your favorite modeling style and why?

_____

_____

_____

_____

_____

What are two styles of fashion you would like to focus on and why?

_____

_____

_____

_____

_____

7

Modeling Tips to Slay the Runway

My journey as a runway model is very exciting, intriguing, and insightful. I have had the pleasure of walking in over 40 fashion shows. I don't fit into the standard category of a runway model because my measurements are height 4'11", chest 41", waist 38", hips 52", weight 185 pounds. Industry standards are height 5'8"-5'10", chest 32"-36", waist 22"-26", hips 33"-35", Weight 110-130 pounds. So how did I make it so far, being in so many shows? Great question! Glad you asked. Here are some reasons why I've been chosen to be in so many shows as a runway model:

1. God's favor
2. My confidence
3. Personality
4. Consistency
5. Ability to adapt
6. My look
7. Referrals
8. Accepting some free gigs

9. Networking and connecting with other models
10. Never giving up

Each of the above reasons has a purpose in my life along my journey. Some of the shows were good, and some bad, but all were great experiences that helped me get to the next level and to where I am now.

Here are some runway modeling tips to make note of:

1. Walk with confidence.
2. Keep an eye on your posture, walking style and poses. Square your shoulders, relax your hands, don't swing your arms too much, take long strides, place one foot in front of each other, and strut like nobody's business.
3. Understand the type of walking style the designer is looking for.
4. Remember you are the living hanger that brings the clothes to life.
5. Work the style; don't let the style work you.
6. Don't be so serious. Certain styles give you character.
7. If you fall, get back up, and keep walking. Keep the show moving.
8. Entertain the audience with your personality, but nothing over the top.
9. Take your time on the runway, but not too slow.
10. Become familiar with the clothes you wear on the runway.
11. Don't let nerves get the best of you.
12. Stretch and soak your feet after every show to relax and unwind.
13. Don't forget to eat a meal. Models do eat!
14. HAVE FUN!!!

MODELING TIPS TO SLAY THE RUNWAY

Name some reasons why you believe you were chosen to be in some fashion shows?

1. _____
2. _____
3. _____
4. _____
5. _____

What do you like about runways? Why?

_____

_____

_____

_____

_____

8

Grab Your Passport, Honey!

Now many of you may be shocked about what I'm getting ready to tell you right now. LOLOL I don't think y'all ready. Here goes!

Out of all that modeling and opportunities I've had in my modeling career, I've never traveled outside of CA for any modeling gigs. LOLOLOL Isn't that crazy. When you go to my page on Instagram at @sassyclassymodel, it seems I've been everywhere, right? Not so, but I will say this: it is definitely on my goals list.

I'm so excited to report to y'all, as I'm writing this section, I have #breakingnews (SCREAMING and DANCING with excitement)! I just got picked up to be a plus size/curvy petite model for New York Fashion Week #NYFW #YAYY My flight is booked. My room is set. Words cannot express how excited I am right now. For one year, I kept telling people I will one day be in a fashion show for NYFW, Paris, London, Milan, and others.

Let me tell you, I am big on manifesting the things I desire in my life. I truly believed I would have what I say. I was told, "You are too short and not skinny enough to be in fashion shows for Fashion Week tours." "You must be 5'8" or taller size 4-6." Well, again, I believed the impossible, and yet it has come to past. I will say NYFW is definitely a different experience in terms of walking styles, posing, and personality on the runway. It is a very straightforward walk, uniform, very little posing, little to no personality on the runway. Very different from Los Angeles style. Always learn the different styles of walking so you can be versatile wherever you go.

Here are other tips to traveling out-of-state as a model: be sure to apply for a passport or visa. Having a visa especially is very important because it allows you to work as a model in that particular country. Always have your portfolio available for potential clients to view. Network as much as possible since you never know who you may come across along the way. Continue to be cautious about who you book with for your career opportunities out-of-state if you are not going directly through an agency.

Some key nuggets per state travel location, based on what I've read or experienced:

Los Angeles

Now, I live in Los Angeles, California, at the moment, so I have the tea. #baby I will say that there are numerous opportunities in LA. However, you just have to go after what you want. LA has a different walking style from most other fashion states. In most cases, you can show a lot of personality on the runway, but it's different per designer or show. Be sure to double check before you look like you're doing too much. LA is somewhat laid-back, but a lot of times you can book more based on your talents depending on how you showcase it. LA is very expensive in terms of living. in case you are planning to station yourself in LA. It just seems as if every time you turn around, you are being taxed on something. Then you think, where did all my money go? #idontknow Because there are so many opportunities in LA, it's possible you can experience being in commercials or movies or even become a brand ambassador, model in numerous runway shows whether they are small or big. So, girl, don't be afraid to go make that money. Opportunity awaits you! (Saying this in my Darth Vader voice) #LOLOL'

Date you traveled to Los Angeles

_____

For what purpose did you travel?

_____

_____

_____

_____

New York

New York is a jackpot for high-fashion brands, magazines, photographers, stylists, and marketing. NY is high-paced, Honey, so don't get left behind. It's very business-oriented and professional, and they don't tolerate tardiness. Respect people's time, and have a positive attitude. The way you present yourself will go a long way. You must be on your Ps and Qs.

Date you traveled to New York

_____

For what purpose did you travel?

_____

_____

_____

_____

Asia

Can you say GUARANTEED CONTRACTS??? I can't hear you!!! (Laughing) Asia is one of the locations that have a contract that guarantee a certain amount of earnings for a period of time, depending on your experience as a model. This process happens through an agency. Always be sure to check the fine print to negotiate the best price.

Date you traveled to Asia

_____

For what purpose did you travel?

_____

_____

_____

_____

Mexico

Mexico is a great place to build your portfolio. Speaking Spanish is a plus. There are more magazine opportunities and local campaigns for advertising. They are not as strict on body measurements, and there is great scenery.

Date you traveled to Mexico

_____

For what purpose did you travel?

_____

_____

_____

_____

London

London is stricter in terms of modeling. Determine the type of model you would like to become. Scout for a reputable agency to help you advance in your modeling career. Study the walking style of London modeling to become more familiar with how the models walk on the runway. Always practice posing to make sure you are on point. Have your portfolio available for potential clients' view. Make sure your social media is up to par. Your physical appearance and health are very important.

Date you traveled to Los Angeles

_____

For what purpose did you travel?

_____

_____

_____

Paris

Paris just sounds so lovely. I would love to model in Paris! The laws are very different in Paris when it comes to modeling, so be sure you do as much research as possible. The minimum age requirement to model is 16. Try to go through an agency for modeling opportunities. If you go through an agency and you are younger than 16, the agency should know what steps to take next. In Paris as a model, you are considered an employee versus a contractual worker. RED ALERT! RED ALERT! #beware Taxes are high in Paris for models; as a result, models only receive 33% of their total earnings (subject to change). Be sure to have experience in modeling before traveling to Paris. This is the expectation of many of the agencies in this location.

Date you traveled to Paris

For what purpose did you travel?

GRAB YOUR PASSPORT, HONEY!

_____

_____

Feel free to explore more about these locations and others. Some destinations may be a better fit for you than others. Always, always read the fine print of every contract. Gain fashion marketing experience to know what you are up against. Whatever direction you decide to go, be sure to be consistent, persistent, and focused. Always remember, safety first. Network with other models to build genuine relationships and connections. You got this, so don't you dare try to give up.

9

Brand Ambassador

What is a brand ambassador?

A brand ambassador is a model who markets and advertises a designer's clothing line or product.

Some of the duties of a brand ambassador

Advertise and post on social media, attend clients' events, engage with the audience, get to know the brand, be creative with showcasing the brand, etc.

Where to find clients to be their brand ambassador

You can find potential clients for you to represent their brand by reaching out directly to that brand. Advertise a brand's product or piece of clothing and tag them to get your foot in the door. Clients will reach out to you directly by word of mouth via social media or if your contact information is given out.

BRAND AMBASSADOR

How to become a brand ambassador?

1. Decide what type of brand ambassador you would like to be.
2. Create an ambassador program for yourself to provide a list of your services to potential clients.
3. Determine your price point. It should make sense. Some tips of what your price should include the following:
4. Professional pictures/photographer/videographer
5. Your time
6. Creativity
7. Travel time or location
8. Makeup, hair, & other necessities
9. Other potential items that would help to market the brand for the client
10. Research the brand you desire to represent to determine if you would like to move forward.
11. Create or use an electronic service that provides ambassador contract documentation that you can customize as needed per client with all the legal jargon requiring signatures from both parties. Be sure to get clarity from the client on their preference for your hair, nails, makeup, and shoes. Would they like you to have any special props to create the customer experience, location setting, etc.?
12. Once the client hires you and the contract is signed, let's work!
13. Post according to the time frame established, listing the client's website or other useful information for customers to purchase the item(s) you are advertising.
14. Keep track of how well you are doing in your program to know what areas need improvement.
15. MAKE IT FUN! HAVE FUN!

I have to tell you, being a brand ambassador is so much fun! I will get into why, but let me tell you, I am a brand ambassador for more than 20 brands. Yassssssss!!!! Now, don't get scared or intimidated by this because girl, I started at zero. Then my zero became one. Then one became two. Then the requests to be a brand ambassador just kept multiplying, and it continues. Can you believe that!!!! #iamindemand

Some of the reasons why I like being a brand ambassador is that I get to showcase my personality, create fun and amazing content, make new connections, grow in the area of enhancing my marketing and advertising, make some MONEY, market myself and open the door for more opportunities, and inspire others to do the same!

Being a brand ambassador is time consuming, but it is very rewarding.

Look at you, doing so good! How you doin'!!! You betta' go ahead now! You made it to through session 2. Pat yourself on the back, and tell yourself you are awesome!

SESSION 3

SPEAKING MY SELF-CARE LANGUAGE

10

Your Self-Care Royalty

It's important as a model you take care of yourself. I didn't know what self-care was, let alone meant, until I met Natasha McCrea, the CEO & Founder of Love CEO Academy. She is one of my business coaches. Day in and day out, I would consistently hustle, grind, and support others while I neglected myself. I realized I was so exhausted from everything that my body begin to shut down physically. When you have beat your body up so much from all the non-stop working, let me tell you, your body will send you a message so you get the point. I felt like my body was telling me, "Girl you betta' get somewhere and sit down, reset, and recharge." LOLOL Natasha offers a "self-care" program. Being a part of her program has allowed me to realize I needed to include self-care and self-love in my life. As a result of going through her program, I now have a continuous self-care day on my calendar each week. It involves, giving myself a home spa royalty treatment, playing video games, ordering my favorite meal, speaking words of affirmation into my life, praying, relaxing on the couch, and sleeping. Yasss, Honey, I make sure I take care of myself now! Don't punish yourself for taking care of the very thing that keeps you going after what you want. Your health is important. Never forget that.

Times may be a little hectic when you may not get enough sleep with other responsibilities outside your journey. Self-care allows you to recharge, reset, and refresh. Pace yourself. If you don't take of you, no one else will. There are various self-care routines you can do to balance your life. Your self-care routine doesn't have to be strenuous, but whatever you decide, be sure to be consistent. It can be simple but customized to you. Make it fun! Post your self-care plan on your wall or mirror to remind yourself each day that taking care of you is most important before you can take care of anyone else.

Some examples are the following:

- Praying
- Acupuncture
- Massage
- Pedicure
- Manicure
- Time at the gym
- Walk somewhere peaceful
- Time at the beach
- Time being quiet and relaxing
- Journal in your diary
- Movie or your favorite meal
- Video games
- Going out and having a good time
- Sleep for 6-8 hours

- Stretch
- Long spa bath
- Doing absolutely nothing
- Practice saying, "no" or "yes," depending on your challenge
- Speaking words of affirmations
- Choose YOU

Do you have a self-care plan? _____

If you do not have a self-care plan, create one that is custom to you. Let's create one.

Does your self-care plan consist of spiritual, physical, emotional, and mental care? _____

What is your self-care plan for--spiritual, physical, emotional, and mental care?

_____

_____

_____

_____

_____

_____

YOUR SELF-CARE ROYALTY

What is your weekly self-care plan?

_____

_____

_____

_____

_____

_____

How often do you, or will you, do self-care?

_____

Are you willing to be consistent with your plan?

_____

How will you remember to give yourself self-care royalty (i.e., keep it on your calendar, post it on your wall, etc.)?

_____

_____

_____

_____

_____

_____

Always remember,

> *"My self-love is the guide to every right decision.*
> *Everything you desire is wrapped in your self-love."*
>
> —Natasha McCrea

11

Self-Development & Evaluation

<u>Strengths</u>

Identify the strengths you possess and utilize it in the industry. You can transform your strengths into great ways of being more creative, efficient, and fresher in perspective in the modeling industry. Now don't get to comfortable thinking just because you have a strength, you can't easily lose it. It's possible if you don't continue to build on that strength. We've all heard the saying before, "Use it, or lose it." Yeah, that's right, so keep growing what you were gifted with.

What are your strengths?

_____

_____

_____

Weaknesses

Many like to think they don't have weaknesses or, rather, throw them out of their minds, but be real with yourself, Honey. Identifying your weaknesses allows you to come to terms with your internal struggle. It's up to you to put action to it, so you can bring forth growth in your mental and physical journey. Don't treat them as disadvantages because they are advantages. Ok, let me give you an example. If your weakness is walking in heels, what should you do? Girl, go out, buy you some heels, strap them on, and practice walking in your heels in your living room, dining room, kitchen, the grocery store, wherever. You gotta do what you gotta do to make your weakness your strength.

What are your weaknesses?

_____

_____

_____

Opportunities

Point to three people and say with authority and excitement in your voice, "You get an opportunity." "You get an opportunity." "You get an opportunity." Now point to yourself and say, "I get an opportunity." #yassss There are so many opportunities out there for everyone that goes out there and gets them. Say this with me: "I have exponential growth and exposure in the modeling industry to attract larger opportunities to enhance what I deserve." Propel yourself to move forward and go after what you

SELF-DEVELOPMENT & EVALUATION

want. #periodt (Refer to the "Opportunities Galore" chapter for how to find opportunities

Threats

Wow, that model walks so good; I could never be that good. She has the best poses which I will never be able to do. I have so much cellulite; I would feel embarrassed to wear a bathing suit. I have so much acne on my face; I'm not as beautiful as her. Just STOP. DON'T create unnecessary threats that will sabotage your growth as a model. Threats bring about fear, and fear keeps you stagnant and left behind. Tackle your threats that implant your mind with negative thoughts. Listen: you will be just fine. Stay focused.

What do you see as potential threats?

_____

_____

_____

12

Mindset: The Power of the Mind

There is a price to pay for your dreams. There will be some losses and wins, but no matter what, never give up. There are times I felt like giving up because more money was going out than coming in. Sometimes I didn't have money for things like gas, food, makeup, additional clothing requested, and I was mentally depleted. I asked myself, *Is this journey of modeling worth it?* I answered myself, *Yes, because every opportunity I've been blessed with on this journey, my return is greater than my lack.* Great things are worth fighting for. Someone is always watching you. You are an inspiration to someone, so make sure you represent yourself well. Do not speak defeat, self-hate, or doubt into who you are. Negativity will only leave you behind.

Be mindful of the company you entertain and ask yourself, "Does this environment help better me?" If not, you need to change your circle. Get rid of toxic people and relationships in your life. It can only hurt you in the long run. You will not always receive the support from close friends, loved ones, or others you depend on for support. This is part of your journey, so don't give up. God will place people in your life that are strangers, give you favor, and bless you more than what you could've ever dreamed of. This is not a popcorn journey, where dreams come true instantly. Be realistic, and give yourself time to grow. If you reach success too fast, it is possible you can risk everything you've earned quickly because you had no lessons in between to know what it took for you to be where you are. Don't be afraid to make mistakes. Mistakes are what make you. Mistakes are great teachers. Lessons learned, then success is earned.

I am a strong believer in words of affirmation, believing God, praying, and speaking things into existence. On this journey, I found myself understanding how important it is for me to believe God for the impossible. Some of my daily routines included reading these words of affirmation by Derrick Jaxn:

> Words of Affirmation......
> Abundance is mine, spiritually and financially.
> My current circumstances do not reflect
> my future overflow. I am sought
> after by opportunity & attractive to success.
> I will inevitably meet wealth & expansion
> in every area of my life.
> Derrick Jaxn

I also pray and ask God that every opportunity HE blesses me with will be a greater purpose than why I believe I attended. Each time, God showed up in ways I would've never expected. Modeling has truly changed my life and increased my faith. Develop a routine to program your mind, so it won't program you. Increase your belief system. It is easy for us to think negative about ourselves before we think positive. Whatever routine you decide to adopt, be consistent, and stay encouraged.

The battle that can take over our life is the battle of our minds. In the famous words of Iyanla Vanzant, "There is no greater battle in life than the battle between the parts of you that want to be healed, the parts of you that are comfortable, and content remaining broken." You cannot afford to stay where you are in a negative mental state. A broken mind can leave you mentally and emotionally bankrupted. Shed the guilt from your life, so you can be free. Don't allow people's opinions and actions to control the direction of your life. Set boundaries and stick to them. Always remember, your mindset is food for the soul.

Your Value

Say this: "I AM VALUABLE." Sometimes in the industry, you will feel like you're being taken advantage of. Well, you must know that you are valuable. If you don't value you, no one else will. Don't be afraid to state your value once you gain more experience. You deserve to be paid for your career. Your value also depends on you being authentic and speaking out when you feel uncomfortable. Sometimes, we try so hard to fit in with the crowd. People respect you more for being the real you. You know you were born a leader. So, why walk as a follower when you have the birthright of being a leader? Take the lead on your life.

13

Trusting Yourself

Trust Starts Within

Trust goes a long way. Trusting yourself to fulfill your dreams gives yourself permission to win. Always remember you are your own enemy. Do not stay stuck in your head in believing something that you are not. You are what you say you are. You are the architect of your own life. Trust yourself in building the life you deserve.

Do you trust yourself to continue to go after your dreams?

_____

_____

_____

_____

What confirmation allows you to believe you trust yourself?

___

___

___

___

___

The 5 C's to Live By

Character – Your character goes a long way. How are you portraying yourself? What is your personality? Your character is your loyalty, behavior, honesty, and much more. Are you an influencer? Don't be afraid to show your personality on stage, behind the scenes, and outside of your profession. Be mindful of how you conduct yourself. At the end of the day, who are you representing?

Describe your character

___

___

___

TRUSTING YOURSELF

_____

_____

Confidence – Are you confident in who you are and what you're doing? If not, you need to find a way to build your confidence. In this industry, people are attracted to those that are confident in who they are. Confidence shows your strength, being unafraid to face challenges that may arise. You have to have the attitude, "You either like me, or you don't." Don't look to be accepted where you're not wanted. Some will like you, and some won't. Don't look to be validated by people that don't value you. Stand strong and firm in everything you do. Always do your best.

Are you confident in who you are? Yes/No _____

If you are not confident in who you are, are you willing to change the things you can change? Yes/No _____

Commitment – How committed are you to becoming a model? Are you willing to make unexpected sacrifices? Your commitment to the industry will be tested often. If you are not committed, you will quit easily, and this is not the industry for you. When you are committed, you will keep going no matter what difficult obstacles come your way. Commitment shows how dedicated you are to fulfilling your dreams.

How committed are you to taking your modeling career to the next level?

_____

_____

_____

_____

_____

Where do you desire to be two years from now?

_____

_____

_____

_____

_____

Consistency – Are you "sometimey"? How often are you focused on your mission to achieve your modeling vision and desires? How bad do you want it? Make a vow to yourself that you will stay focused no matter what. You should adopt a method that gives you a routine of how you tackle this journey. For example, if you need to work on finding modeling opportunities, set a schedule of

TRUSTING YOURSELF

how many you will look for every day, week, or month. Make sure you keep track and do your follow-up. Most people fail because of their lack of consistency. Be intentional. What helps you to stay consistent?

_____

_____

_____

_____

_____

Charisma – Are you charming? Do you inspire anyone? Have the mindset to unite people together if it's doable. People enjoy following you when you inspire them in some form, do things for a cause, and possess some form of leadership. You will find some people are drawn to you naturally because of your personality. Develop your people skills. You will definitely need them in this industry.

Do you have the charisma to bring people together? Why?

_____

_____

_____

_____

I knew you wouldn't give up! You made it through session 3. I'm so proud of you! Time for another celebration song. Ayeeee!! Put on that song by Post Malone, "Congratulations (feat. Quava)." Now dance, and show what you got!

Session 4

GIRL, I GOT THE TEA

14

Resolution to the Lies & Scams

What the Industry Is Not Telling You

Let me talk to you for a minute. I want you to listen very closely. There are some people out there that are intentionally trying to do you harm in any way possible. Don't believe the smoke and mirrors. Now, don't get me wrong. Modeling is so much fun, but there are pros and cons to everything.

When I first started off in the industry, I didn't know what I didn't know. The more opportunities I receive, the more I learn about the industry. I can think of one experience that made me so mad. So, you guys know, I represent a lot of brands now, but that wasn't always the case. I saw an opportunity posted on Instagram to be a hair model. I told my daughter about it and asked her whether she wanted to be a hair model as well. She said, "Yes." The post seemed legit. I scanned the business page looking at past post. I was feeling more and more confident about the opportunity. The post said to DM them if interested, so I did.

RESOLUTION TO THE LIES & SCAMS

They reached out to me saying, we have two more slots available to be a hair brand ambassador. I inquired about the benefits of being a hair brand ambassador. They said that each model selected would be responsible for posting themselves wearing the wigs/hair, receiving 50% off on any future orders and a free human hair lace wig given to each model once a week to help advertise. The model would need to pay only a one-time fee of $80 to cover some of the shipping. Once the models are selected and agree, each would be added to a group chat on Instagram, listing all the other important details. I said, "Ok. Sounds pretty fair to me." I agreed. They sent me their CashApp, and I sent $80 each for my daughter and myself, which is a total of $160.

Then after sending the money, I realized I didn't check to see if they had a website on their page. I was thinking, *How are we going to select the wigs we want to wear?* I reached out to them to inquire about their website. Do you know what they told me? "We don't have a website. That's why the pictures are posted on our page for you to select." I said, "It doesn't give you all the details about the hair or anything. It's just models and mannequins advertising the hair." They said, "Exactly, that's all you need." I said, "WHAT????? That doesn't make sense!!!!" I then said, "Well, not everyone has a website for their business."

Then my daughter and I started looking them up on the internet under the business name used on their Instagram. Do you know what we found out? They had scammed others, and a person made a whole video on YouTube about how they were scamming people, others would report them, and then they start a new page under a different name, all to scam people out of their money. The person that exposed them on YouTube also said the pictures look very real on their page, but it is only pictures from other companies to make the hair look legit. My mouth and heart dropped. I looked further on their page, and all their comments were turned off for each post. #SMH

Without me telling them I just discovered all of this, I reached out to them saying that I changed my mind and that I'm requesting a refund. Guess what they told me? "No refunds allowed! You should've never sent your money." I became so angry and upset that I just lost $160 on a stupid scam because I didn't do proper research. I tried to stop the transaction through my bank stating I've just been scammed, and they said that since it came from a third-party app (CashApp) the money is not insured. Therefore, they were not be able to refund me or stop the transaction because it was already sent. They said, I would need to go directly to CashApp to dispute. I had no success through CashApp either because there are no live representatives. I gave up and exhausted all my options and decided to just accept I just had been scammed. Now, I check #everything.

In spite of any cons to the industry, some of the greatest rewards I received was due to me never giving up, sacrificing my time often without pay, improving my knowledge in the industry, perfecting my walking style, and gaining more confidence. Always stay in solution mode.

| Behind the Scenes | Possible Resolution |

RESOLUTION TO THE LIES & SCAMS

You are sometimes not fed prior or after the fashion show.	Get a bite to eat before call time.
You are rarely paid or not at all.	Give yourself a cut-off period as to when you will no longer work for free.
Sometimes you don't receive your photos for the fashion show.	Meet the photographers before the show start and exchange information. Bring your personal photographer with you, if permitted.
Sometimes when you're picked to be in the fashion show, the designer(s) may not have anything for you to wear for the show. You won't be able to walk in the show, which can cost you time and money.	Ask the event coordinator in charge, prior to the show, whether there are any designers that fit your size, or whether there is a fitting rehearsal.
Show is disorganized with few or no instructions.	Ask the event coordinator whether there are specific details you should know prior to the show (e.g., rehearsals, designer walking order, etc.)
You receive nothing in return (No pictures, clothing, pay, etc.)	Try to negotiate with the designer to see whether they are willing to give you one of

	their clothing items in exchange for your time.
Some makeup artists are unable to match your skin tone.	Bring your own makeup as a backup. See whether it is okay to come makeup ready. Ask the makeup artist, whether they are able to match your skin tone.
Models are required to sell a certain number of tickets for the show in order to model in the show. Often, if you do not sell the required amount of tickets, you are responsible for paying for the tickets you didn't sell. Tickets may be $40 per person or more, and you may be required to sell 3 - 5. Do the math. The estimated amount would be $120 - $200.	Ask yourself these questions: Is it feasible? Do I want to take on this responsibility? What am I receiving in return? Is it worth it?
Photographers and designers often have a disagreement on their pay, while models are caught in the middle trying to figure out how to get some form of compensation.	Try to negotiate with the designer to see whether they are willing to give you one of their clothing items in exchange for your time.

RESOLUTION TO THE LIES & SCAMS

SCAMS!!! There are so many posted modeling opportunities that appear to look real, but they are sometimes disguises to lure you into stealing your money, sex trafficking, or being drugged, raped, or worse. Predators know models will sometimes do anything to become a model, so they prey on desperate individuals.	Some of the ways of knowing whether an opportunity is real or not include following a social media account called, @nopaynorunway, a Facebook group for Los Angeles models, where they post examples of how people have tried to scam them. You can also google and research "common runway modeling scams." Be careful. Some people are not who they say they are.

Stay in Safety Mode

We often hear, "Safety first." Well, it is so true, and it is important to take heed that safety always comes first. What good is a gig if your life is gone because you didn't look at the warning signs or listen to your first instincts. No gig is worth losing your life. Always remember the following:

- Never go alone to a photographer's home, which is sometimes their studio, for a photoshoot unless there are others present such as makeup artist, stylist, other models, etc.
- Meet up in public places.
- If you feel uncomfortable, LEAVE.
- Keep your phone well charged prior to going to a gig just in case anything happens.

- Do not take any drinks from stranger, unless it is sealed and you know what you are drinking.
- Make sure your electronics, such as cellphones, laptops, iPads, etc., are insured just in case they are stolen at a casting call, modeling rehearsal, photoshoot, fashion show, or other places.
- Make someone aware of where you are going if you will be going by yourself.
- If you are harmed in any way or taken advantage of, make sure you report it immediately to get help for yourself and possibly prevent harm from happening to others.
- Always carry at least one of these items on hand: pepper spray, taser, Swiss knife, GPS tracker, stun gun, or other useful items.
- Take a self-defense class.
- If abducted, act like a wild animal. Pretend to have an asthma attack or seizure.

15

Won't Stop, Can't Stop Learning

Be a continuous student of your industry. Study the modeling industry to educate yourself, so that you become familiar with exactly what you are getting into. Learn the top paid models in the industry, their story, how they accomplished what they accomplished, how they strut on the runway, pros and cons of the industry, modeling terminology, changes in the industry, top designers, photographers, popular modeling magazines, important trainings, and more. You want to always stay current and know what you're talking about. It will help you on your journey by setting you apart from just being a model. What are some things you recently learned about modeling that you didn't know before?

1. _____

2. _____

3. _____

4. _____

5. _____

6. _____

7. _____

8. _____

9. _____

10. _____

16

Modeling Etiquette: Your Reputation Precedes You

How you conduct yourself—your behavior, following instructions, overall work ethic, and being pleasant—will take you very far. If you are being disruptive, have a hard time listening or arrive late to shows that have time restrictions, it is likely that you will not get a call back. Guess what? The industry is small, so word will travel fast and follow you everywhere you go.

Here are some examples of incorrect modeling etiquette (Can you think of some examples of correct modeling etiquette? Fill in the blanks)

- **Incorrect modeling etiquette**: A designer reaches out to you to arrange a fitting. You let them know you will be there at the time arranged. Well, when the date & time arrive, you cancel at the last minute, don't show up, or don't take it seriously because you're not getting paid. You then decide to reach out to the designer two days later, requesting to reschedule. REALLY!!!???

Correct modeling etiquette:

_____

_____

- **Incorrect modeling etiquette**: The call time for models for the show is 11 a.m., but you decide to show up at 3 p.m. because that's what you want to do. You don't communicate with the designer to let them know in advance, either.

    Correct modeling etiquette:

    _____

    _____

- **Incorrect modeling etiquette**: While the designer is trying to give instructions to the models for the show, you decide to hold an additional conversation with another model at the same time.

    Correct modeling etiquette:

    _____

    _____

MODELING ETIQUETTE: YOUR REPUTATION PRECEDES YOU

Always check your attitude. You can easily get cut at any time for unacceptable modeling etiquette and behavior. You are not the only one with your talent. You are replaceable.

17

Modeling Industry Standards

Do Age, Height, Weight, or Race Matter in This Industry?

In my experience, "yes" and "no." It depends on the requirements of the show. Sometimes there are strict stipulations, such as specific age, height, and sometimes location. There have been cases when a certain height was required; however, the designer liked my personality, walking style, mannerism, and confidence. So I was chosen. I am nowhere near the stereotypical height, weight, or age requirements for the standard modeling industry. I stand at 4'11", 41 years old, plus size, Black, beautiful, and confident. I know who I am. I don't have to hide it. If you manage to make a name for yourself, a lot of the requirements they are requesting can be irrelevant for you. If you are what they are looking for, the designer will make it work for you. It would then be possible; you would then be in demand!

If I Have a Disability, Can I Still Be a Model?

Having a disability shouldn't stop you from being a model if that is truly your passion. I've learned since being in the modeling industry, the industry is changing from the norm and is gravitating to diversity. Diversity gives the designers and audience possibilities and vision. The world is not one dimensional, so why does the industry have to be? No matter what challenge you face, always bring YOU to the table in everything that you do.

Yasss! I see you were built for this because you are still going and made it through session 4! Now that's what I'm talking about!!!! Let's see what session 5 has in store for you.

Session 5

IDENTITY CHECK

18

Don't Chase the Hype; Chase the Dream

Don't be quick to accept every opportunity that comes your way. There will be more. Don't get caught up in the fear of loss. Social media paints the picture that everything falls in place all the time, and it's a seamless process. LIES! LIES! LIES! WAKE UP, and come back to reality. Nothing is perfect, so embrace the good and bad. Many times, the pace of your journey is contingent upon the accessibility of your resources, finances, circumstances in your life, and your ability to keep dreaming no matter what you face. Whatever you desire to do has to make sense. If you create the hype, be able to back it up with authenticity. You are a role model to many, so don't create false narratives to appear something you're not. Every false narrative will be exposed at some point in your life, so the hype can only get you so far. Everyone's dream is customized to their personal path and journey.

19

Social Media Elevation

Instagram Tips for Your Modeling Page

Create a personal Instagram page strictly for modeling to represent you and your story. Your modeling page shouldn't consist of pizza, politics, your favorite car, etc. unless you are modeling for a brand that represents the message or product. Here are some key steps:

- Write down a list of possible Instagram handles for your page that are catchy, unique, and represent you. Try to include the word *model* if possible. Have fun!
- Your profile picture should stand out. If it does, it will attract people to your page.
- When you make your first post, it should make a statement of who you are.
- Make your page public so you can get exposure. There are really no secrets once you enter the world of social media. You

can always block or remove yourself from a tagged post. You never know who you will inspire just by being you.
- Post a variety of your modeling events, such as videos of you walking the runway, backstage footage, pictures with other models. Share your story and authentic moments.
- Download cellphone apps to manage your Instagram page and to understand what attracts your followers: *Follower Analyzer, Followers & Unfollowers, Font Candy,* & *Blastup*.
- You can promote yourself through Instagram promotions, which allow you to advertise yourself. Price range may vary.
- If you have other accounts, you can link all your accounts into one. Google for instructions.
- Your Instagram page can sometimes be used in the place of your Comp Card, depending on the casting instructions.
- Build your Instagram with photoshoots, fashion shows, magazine print, etc.
- When posting pictures on your social media, if someone else took the picture other than you, always be sure to give them credit by mentioning their name and social media information.
- Always be mindful of how you are representing yourself. For example, if you desire to be in a teen magazine, it is not a good idea to have sexual content or simulate sexual positions. That attracts the wrong audience and can cause you to miss valuable opportunities.
- Have a message in your post that captures your audience. Some will like only your picture, and others will read your message *and* like your picture. Don't get too caught up in the likes; however, the likes also tell you what your audience is interested in.

- Study your social media algorithms, insights overviews, and your audience engagement.
- Know that people follow hashtags, so when selecting hashtags for your post, pick hashtags that have large followings, make sense, and relate to your message in your post. Also, create your own hashtag of your Instagram name. For example, my Instagram handle is @sassyclassymodel. My hashtag is #sassyclassymodel. This will allow anyone that is searching Instagram to pull up all your photos you've hash tagged.
- A social media post should include the following: Your message, the name of the location, credit to any designers, photographers, videographers, makeup artists, others that should have credit, and your choice of hashtags. Do not go hashtag crazy. The maximum hashtags allowed on Instagram right now is 30, but to the number may change depending on the app. Do not try to reach 30 hashtags for every post. Be sure to have spacing in your post (e.g., message, 5 spaces, credit to individuals, 3 spaces, and hashtags). Add the post to your story on your social media as well. Make it fun.
- Who to follow on Instagram? Type in key words like, *modeling*, *magazines*, *designers*, *stylist*, *clothing stores*, etc." You can also go to their following list to see who they are following and follow the individuals of your choice as well. The main goal is not how many followers you can receive but knowing the consistent content you want to see when you're on your social media.

Photo Quality vs. Quantity

Your Instagram page is a reflection of who you are. Someone is always viewing your page, so be creative, and showcase who you are within that profession and your journey. Since someone is always viewing your page, the quality of your photos is very important. When potential designers or well-known companies are scouting for models, they look to see if you invest your money into taking quality pictures. Content is important.

Quantity is important because it reflect the magnitude of your work and consistency in posting new material. You should post at least once or twice a day, or every 4 hours. If you post too often in one day, your reviewers will not be able to see all the material you are posting due to the Instagram algorithm rotation.

20

Facing Rejection, My Closest Enemy

Rejection is part of your journey. It is not the time to give up or quit. If you don't experience rejection, you will never work harder to accomplish what you're trying to reach. Rejection allows you to be a better version of yourself, build your confidence, and help you to have tough skin. DO NOT become depressed, extremely sad, or angry when you are not picked for a fashion show or any opportunity you were attempting you get. MOVE ON, AND LET IT GO. Think of it this way: every "NO" gets you closer to your "YES." The modeling industry can be cutthroat. Everything doesn't come easy. If it did, you would never be the person you are today.

Name some modeling opportunities in which you were rejected & how they made you feel? Include the date as well, if you like.

FACING REJECTION, MY CLOSET ENEMY

1.

2.

3.

4.

5.

21

Don't Stand in the Way of Your Dreams

Be more than just a model. God has given me so many gifts and talents. I am a businesswoman that helps people make multiple streams of income and live out my dreams. I am a homemade chef, soon publishing my cookbook. I dance and do sign language interpretation. I can help pretty much anyone that is just getting started with their business. I am a motivational and inspirational speaker. I am into trading stocks, bonds, foreign currency, futures, options, etc. At one point in my life, I even was part of an organization that helped feed millions of children across the United States. I have 17 years' experience in payroll and 7 years' experience in human resources (experienced in all areas under the umbrella of HR; event planning, workers' comp, 401K, employee relations, etc.), architectural engineering experience, three degrees. I mentor individuals interested in getting into the modeling industry, I'm a single mom of a 19-year-old, and I recently was crowned Ms. California US Nation. My hustle and grind are very real.

When learning to be more than just a model, learn to network. Every part of your journey counts, whether good or bad. I network and attend countless events. It is fun and exciting! Meeting people from all facets of life builds your knowledge, resources, and network. Networking also allows you to get more comfortable with communicating with people on different platforms. You can exchange resources. I truly believe in going out to explore the world and doing what you love. I support a lot of people in their businesses and volunteering my time when I can. Don't have the mindset of expecting something in return, but do it because you desire to from the bottom of your heart. The seeds you plant will not be in vain and will eventually pay off in different forms of blessings. You never know who you may meet that will change your life forever.

You are letting nothing stop you. Do you hear me, girl? Yassss!! You knocked down another session and counting! It's time for another song. Put on that song by Fat Joe, Remy Ma, Jay Z (feat. French Montana, Infared) (clean version) "All The Way Up." Bust your move, and step into session 6.

Session 6

Cash Me on the Go, Honey

22

Model on the Go

Keep Track & Follow-up

Keep a calendar of all your modeling activity. Keep track of all your fashion shows, photoshoots, magazine appearances, print work, etc. You can keep track using a digital (google calendar) or paper (journal, Franklin Covey) calendar. Be sure to follow-up with any potential opportunities approaching that you've been selected for to avoid any conflicts. Specific areas to keep track of include event, location, date, time, distance, designers you're modeling for, and any expenses, bank statements, receipts. (Consult a tax accountant or lawyer for further information.) Sample of tracking:

Event	Runway for Life
Location	458 Main Street, Belva, CA 94025

Date	12/15/19
Time	11am – 8pm
Mileage	20
Designers	Peach Lions
Event Type	Fashion Show
Expenses	$100

Track Your Journey!

List some of your recent events:

#1

Event Name _____

Event Description _____

Location _____

Date _____

Time _____

Mileage _____

Designer(s) _____

Event Type _____

Expenses _____

MODELING BEGINNERS GUIDE

#2

Event Name _____

Event Description _____

Location _____

Date _____

Time _____

Mileage _____

Designer(s) _____

Event Type _____

Expenses _____

MODEL ON THE GO

#3

Event Name _____

Event Description _____

Location _____

Date _____

Time _____

Mileage _____

Designer(s) _____

Event Type _____

Expenses _____

MODELING BEGINNERS GUIDE

#4

Event Name _____

Event Description _____

Location _____

Date _____

Time _____

Mileage _____

Designer(s) _____

Event Type_____

Expenses _____

MODEL ON THE GO

#5

Event Name _____

Event Description _____

Location _____

Date _____

Time _____

Mileage _____

Designer(s) _____

Event Type _____

Expenses _____

#6

Event Name _____

Event Description _____

Location _____

Date _____

Time _____

Mileage _____

Designer(s) _____

Event Type _____

Expenses _____

MODEL ON THE GO

#7

Event Name _____

Event Description _____

Location _____

Date _____

Time _____

Mileage _____

Designer(s) _____

Event Type_____

Expenses _____

23

Budgeting Expenses & Closure

Budget! Budget! Budget! I can't say it enough. I want to caution you that modeling can be very expensive. I have spent so much money in modeling. Some of my expenses include designers' clothing item requests, hair, makeup, standard modeling items, I myself paid to be in a fashion show, driving long distances to rehearsals (gas and mileage), bootcamps, accessories, and the list goes on. Most times, it costs me on average $150 or more per show or modeling event. I've been in about 40+ fashion shows, plus other modeling events. When there is very little return, there is more money going out than coming in when you first start. Funds can get very tight. So decide on a monthly budget, stay disciplined, and focused. This may include you turning down some opportunities if it is not feasible. More will come. Also, you may be able to make your modeling career into a business. There are numerous tax deductions you can write off, such as traveling expenses, food, clothing, etc. Create a separate business bank account specially for business or modeling transactions. You

BUDGETING EXPENSES & CLOSURE

would need an EIN#, etc. Consult a tax advisor for more information. Create a business page on social media along with your website. Don't be afraid to take your modeling career to the next level. Stand up and stand out. You can also inquire about my reference referral contact list to make this a business and writing off taxes. The bottom line is don't let the heart of your passion be the pain to your debt.

Have you developed a budget for your modeling career?

_____

Do you plan on pursuing modeling long-term? If so, why?

_____

_____

_____

_____

_____

Within a month of modeling on average how much have you spent on modeling?

- **Gas $** _____
- **Clothes/Accessories $**_____
- **Hair $** _____
- **Makeup $** _____

- **Modeling Training $** _____

    Total $_____

Looking at your month's worth of expenses, can you survive your modeling career without having a budget?

_____

Have you sought help in your budgeting challenges?

_____

My, my, my, you sho' are killin' it now! Go ahead with yo' bad self. Knocking session by session down! Treat yourself to some delicious tacos covered with everything you like because you deserve it! You are ready for session 7.

Session 7

GIRL, CROSS THAT FINISH LINE

24

Choosing an Agency

What is a Modeling Agency?

A modeling agency is a representation of models in fashion, runway, entertainment, and acting. They handle all the details of the modeling gigs, compensation, contracts, and more.

Dive into the Agency Details

It's important to learn about the person or agency you will be working with. Don't be afraid to get to know who you will be taking the lead on your modeling career. Here are some tips to digest:

- Interview the agency, but always let the agency lead the interview.
- Know why you want to model.
- Never pay to sign with an agency. They get paid when you get booked with various opportunities.
- Ask

CHOOSING AN AGENCY

- How often do you book clients?
- What are your commission rates? Commission amounts are negotiable.
- Can the contract be altered?
- What length of service is required once the contract is signed?
- If I decide to terminate the contract before my term is complete, am I subject to any cancellation fees?
- Do you allow your clients to sign with more than one agency at the same time?
- What territory does your agency cover?
- Can I find some of my own gigs while under contract with your agency?
- How and when do I get paid?
- Do you pay for travel, room, and board?
- Will you issue a 1099 to me at the end of the year for all services rendered?
- Do you book for other opportunities besides modeling?
- What do you offer your clients? (e.g., training, portfolio, Comp Cards, photographers, etc.)

- READ the contract and the FINE print, and don't sign nothing you don't feel comfortable with signing.
- Agency contracts are negotiable.
- GOOGLE the agency!!! GOOGLE the agency!!! GOOGLE the agency!!!
- Research to make sure the agency is legit.
  - View of the model photos.
  - If you visit the location of the agency, travel with someone.
  - Check website link.
  - Are they listed with the Better Business Bureau (BBB)?
- Check the agency reviews.

25

Did I Just Hit a Plateau?

Everyone hits a plateau in their career. Sometimes the repetitive journey becomes boring and can feel stagnant. Does this mean you give up on your passion? The answer is, "No." Here's what you should do: reinvent yourself. How? Sit down and come up with fresh new ideas that will give your modeling career a new unforgettable twist. Here are some ideas. Work behind the scenes instead of always modeling the runway. Acquire and learn a new talent, which would probably help you to be more marketable in other areas as a model. You could also work with a fashion designer to understand more about the fashion world. The bottom line is taking a break for a little bit may allow you to refresh your energy and drive. Either way, don't give up your modeling career if this is what you really desire to do.

26

Opportunities Galore

Out of all the sessions in this book, I believe this session is the session that people will pay most attention to. There are so many ways you can find opportunities for modeling. You just have to be willing to work to find them. Here are some ways you can find opportunities. Reference modeling opportunity referrals and recommendation link will be provided upon inquiry.

- Search reputable modeling casting websites, e.g., www.allcasting.com, www.castingnetworks.com, www.backstage.com, etc. Research the legitimacy of the website before subscribing.
- Sign-up with a modeling agency/firm. I've learned, do not pay to be a part of any firm. They should get paid when you get paid. Review agency contract. Ask as many questions as possible before joining (commission rates, type of jobs they book, start-up costs, etc.). Also see the chapter "Choosing an Agency" for more details.

- Word of mouth or through other models or contacts.
- People may tag you in posts on social media.
- Facebook Modeling Group – some paid gigs.
- Contacts may reach out to you directly.
- Networking events.

List some of your recent opportunities

1. **Opportunity**

   - **Name of the popportunity**

     _____

   - **Where did you find it?**

     _____

   - **Date you attended** _____

2. **Opportunity**

   - **Name of the opportunity**

     _____

   - **Where did you find it?**

     _____

   - **Date you attended** _____

3. **Opportunity**

   - **Name of the opportunity**

     _____

OPPORTUNITIES GALORE

- **Where did you find it?**

  _____

- **Date you attended** _____

4. **Opportunity**

   - **Name of the opportunity**

     _____

   - **Where did you find it?**

     _____

   - **Date you attended** _____

5. **Opportunity #5**

   - **Name of the opportunity**

     _____

   - **Where did you find it?**

     _____

   - **Date you attended** _____

6. **Opportunity**

   - **Name of the opportunity**

     _____

   - **Where did you find it?**

     _____

   - **Date you attended** _____

7. **Opportunity**
   - **Name of the opportunity**

     _____

   - **Where did you find it?**

     _____

   - **Date you attended** _____

I knew all along you had it in you to keep going and never give up. You made it through all the sessions. I am so proud of you! You are ahead of the game! Time for the final victory song. You ready for this? Put on that song by Big Sean, "Why Would I Stop?" You already know what to do!

27

You Made It!

You were designed to soar into your purpose! So show people your heart. Your legacy will live on forever, but if you quit, no one will see who you really are. The worst thing you can do is not to take action in moving forward with your dreams. Nothing stops you but you. What are you waiting for? You were born to walk into your destiny. Don't let your dreams die with you. Give them life!

List Your Modeling 3-year to 5-year Plan - #Goals

1. _____

   _____

   Date achieved _____

2. _____

   _____

Date achieved _____

3. _____
   _____

Date achieved _____

4. _____
   _____

Date achieved _____

5. _____
   _____

Date achieved _____

6. _____
   _____

Date achieved _____

7. _____
   _____

Date achieved _____

PLEASE DO NOT LIMIT YOUR GOALS by only listing your plan here. There's more to your life than this. It doesn't stop here. KEEP GOING!!!

Advanced Tactics

Modeling Consultant Services

If you need more of a personal, one-on-one touch to guide you, just know I am here for you. I offer modeling consultant services that will have you leaping to new levels. Are you ready to leap into posing and runway coaching, confidence and mindset development, jump start your social media page(s), branding yourself, budgeting, building your website, and advancing your career? I'll let you answer that. Don't wait! Packet details are discussed upon inquiry. Visit my website www.confidentcurvess.com, Instagram page at www.instagram.com/sassyclassymodel or @sassyclassymodel, click the link in my bio, and subscribe to learn more about the services I offer. My subscription is FREE!!!!

Modeling Glossary

- **Art Director** – Person responsible for developing the look of an ad, such as editorial or other forms of visual presentation. These individuals consist of either independent contractors or those employed by advertising agencies, magazines, or photographers.

- **Art Model** – A live model posing in front of students for an art class or for a single artist for painting or drawing you in human form.

- **Beauty Shot** – Head shot with makeup and nice hairstyle. The headshot should not be distracting from your overall features.

- **Billing Form** – A form used by models for recording purposes, listing the names of clients, job descriptions, number of hours worked, rate of pay, and all other expenses. The model has the client sign the form, and each of you receives a copy. If an agency is involved, the same process applies.

- **Book** – A model's portfolio book of photos.

- **Booking Conditions** – This consists of booking models for more pay. The booking conditions are established by agencies to outline specific fees such as cancellations (for example, because of bad weather), overtime, weekend fees, bonuses, or other conditions not specified.

- **Booking Out** – Specific hours or days models are unavailable for assignments.

- **Buy Out** – An arrangement in which a client will issue a model a one-time payment for use of their work rather than pay residuals.

- **Call Back** – When a model is called back for a second audition for a final decision.

- **Call Time** – The time set for the model to arrive for the show or event.

- **Commercial Model** – Commercial models that do everything. This isn't normally associated with high fashion, such as a variety types of product ads. (Aaron Marcus, *How to Become a Successful Commercial Model*).

ADVANCED TACTICS

- **Composite** – Comp card used to promote models containing several photos, model stats, and other contact information.

- **Contact Sheet** – Sheet developed by a photographer showing all the shots from a roll of film where photos can be selected quickly and easily. Photos can be black and white or in color.

- **Day Rate** – Rate charged for a model's services for a full eight-hour day of work.

- **Editorial Model** – High fashion models that appear in well-known high-fashion magazines.

- **Editorial Print** – Current trends, clothing, and fashion ideas consisting of fashion pages in a magazine.

- **Fitting** – time spent for a model to try on clothing and outfits for fashion shows, commercials, print shoots, and more.

- **Look Book** – Collection of photos taken of models wearing a designer's or manufacturer's clothing, for fashion editors, clients, buyers, and special customers to show the designers' looks for the season.

- **Mini Book** – Smaller version of portfolio, usually 5x7 inches

- **Runway/Catwalk Model** – Models that walk live runway shows or other types of jobs. Female runway models are minimum 5'10"-5'11"; male runway models, 6'0"-6'2".

- **SED Card** – Another name for composite card.

- **Stats** – Model's height, bust, waist, hips. For men, it's height, chest, and waist. Some measurement requests are subject to change depending on the modeling request.

- **Test** – Test photo shoot paid by the model to test different looks in order to build their portfolio or social media page.

- **TFP (Trade for Prints)** – Model exchange their time to pose for a photographer, and the photographer, in turn, will give the model prints for their portfolio. Typically known as trade for trade.

- **Voucher** – Invoice signed by the model and the client after the model completes a job. The client is billed, and the model can be paid.

Reference websites

- Adorama. (2019, August 2). *How to build a modeling portfolio.* https://www.adorama.com/alc/how-to-build-a-modeling-portfolio

- Helmer, V. (2021, September 28). *Glossary of modeling terms and phrases.* Retrieved from https://www.thebalancecareers.com/list-of-modeling-terms-and-phrases-for-models-2379479

- Ians. (2021, November 12). *Instagram creators can now earn up to $10,000 through Reels.* Business Insider India. https://www.businessinsider.in/tech/news/instagram-will-now-pay-creators-up-to-10000-to-post-reels/articleshow/87664746.cms

- Newman, S. (2018, October 10). *The 10 main types of modeling.* [Blog Post] Retrieved from https://thehhub.com/2018/10/10/types-of-modeling/

Author's Bio

Winner of the Miss Global Noble award, runway model, actress, and founder of Confident Curvess, LLC which she provides exquisite global and virtual modeling consulting services. Damia Gordon double majored in Business and Finance to obtain her Bachelor of Science degree from the University of Phoenix. When she isn't on the catwalk or a movie set, she can be found relaxing at home playing video games, cooking, and gardening.

This West Coast native has taken the modeling industry by storm by defying what we think we know about models, but she's most proud of inspiring others to be unapologetically confident in who they are. She gives credit to God for giving her confidence, wisdom, and positivity, to ignite others' souls to thrive and live again as she tells them, *"Your purpose is brilliant, and your dreams are at stake, so never give up."*

Modeling Picture Album

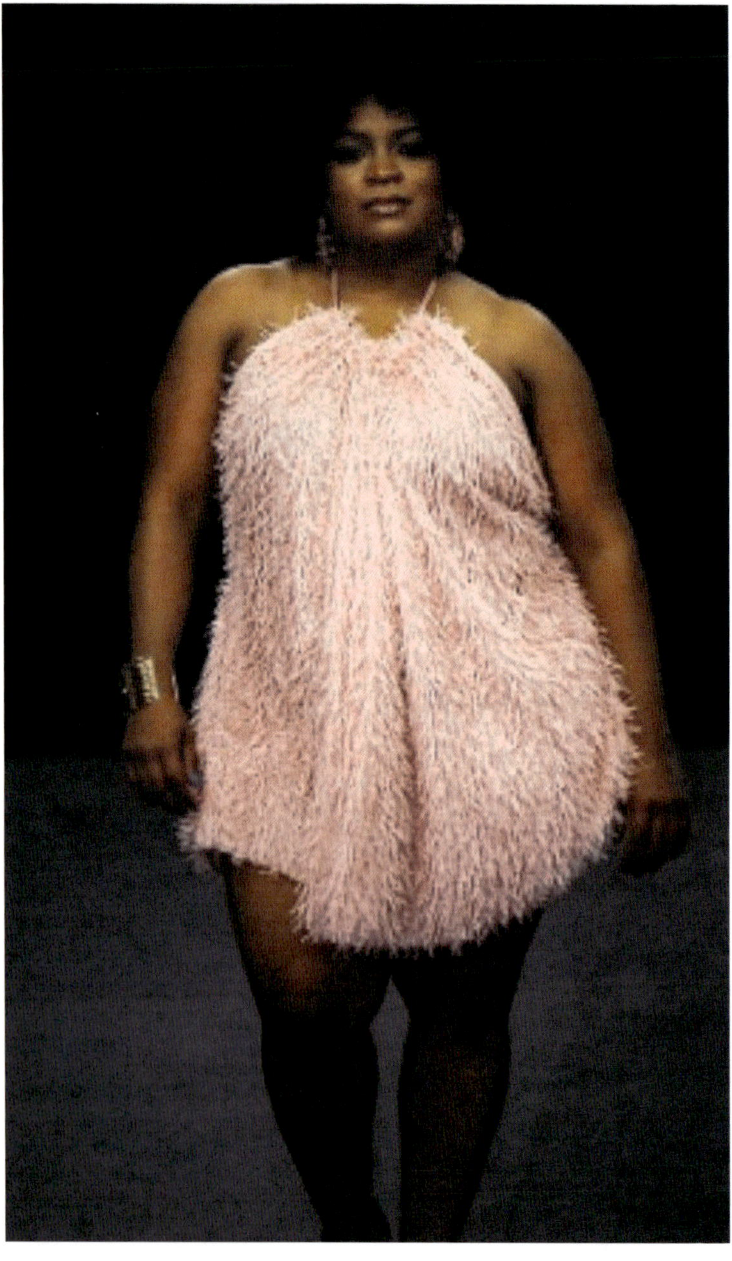

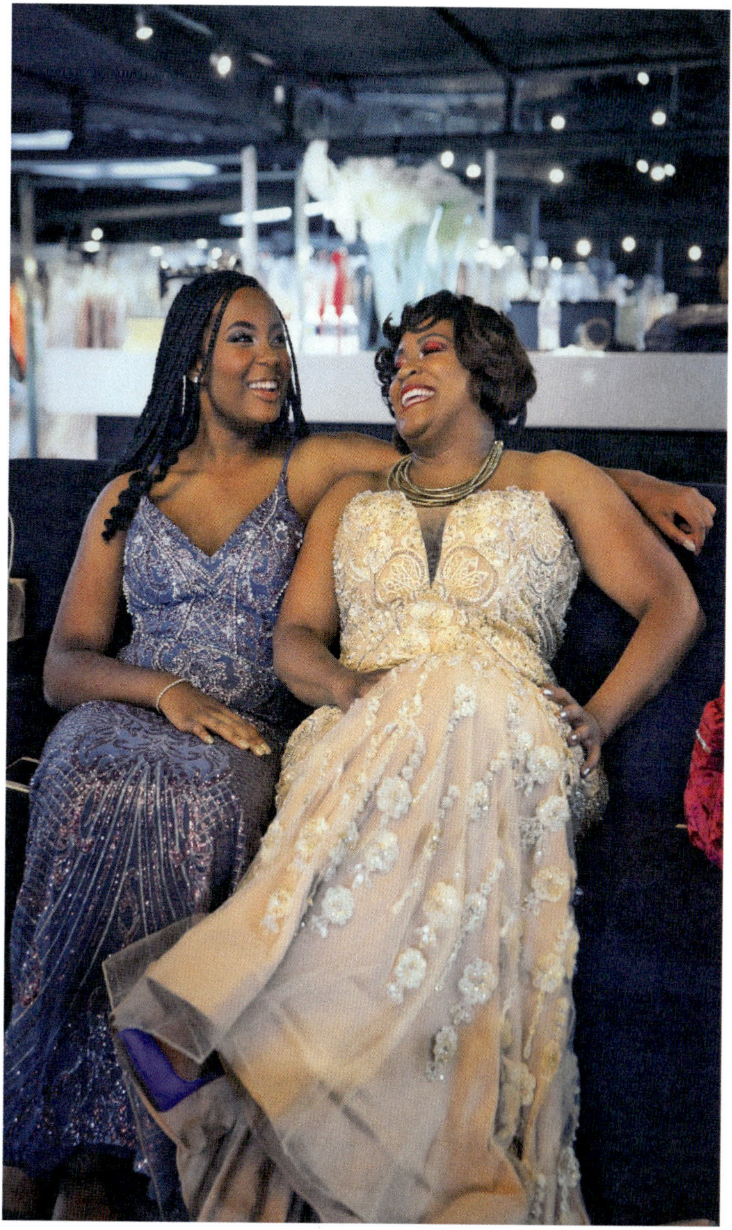

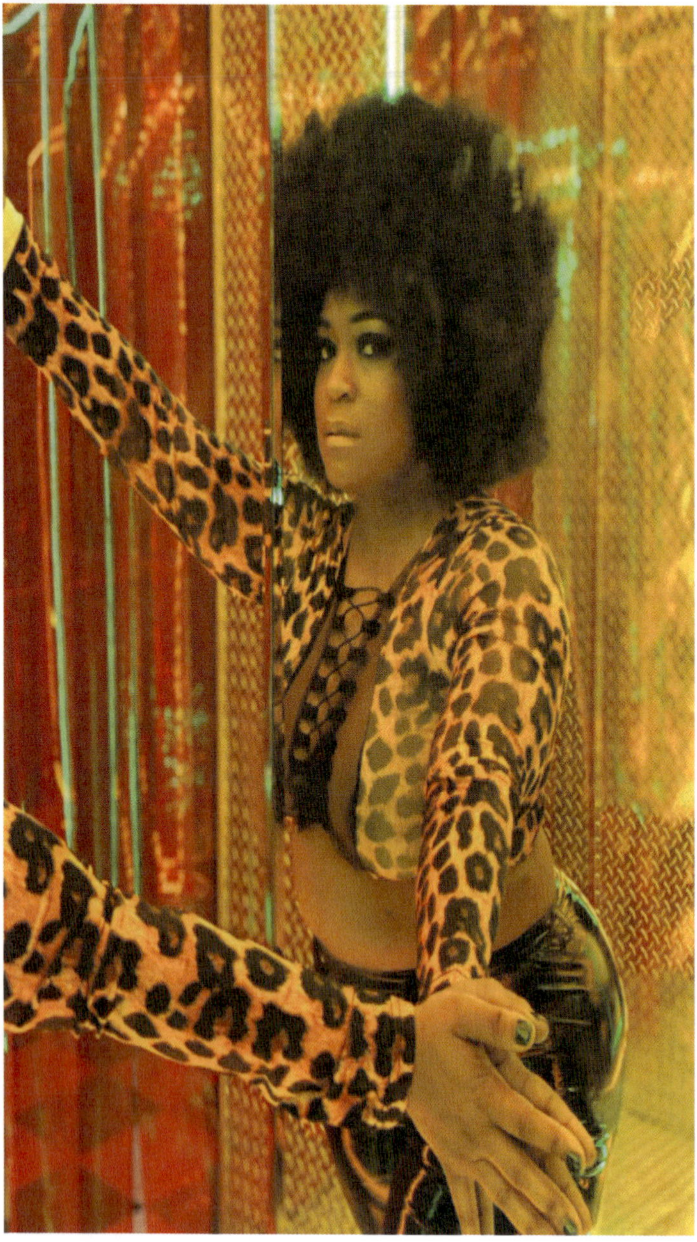

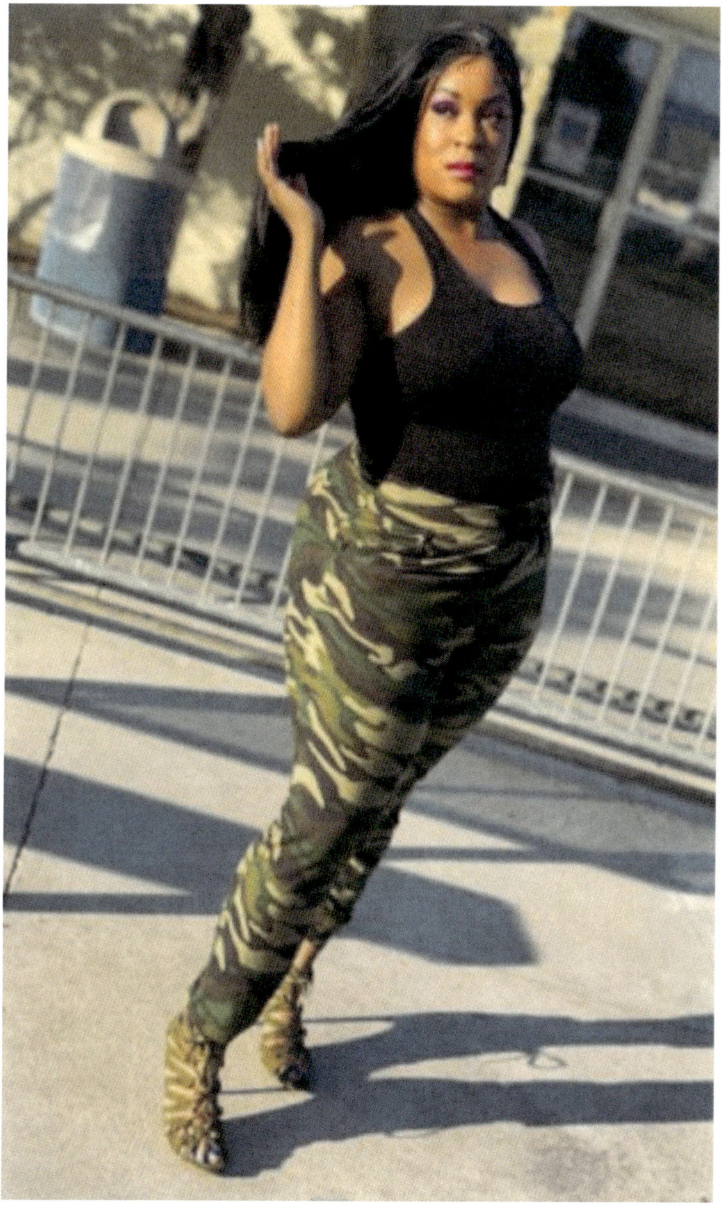

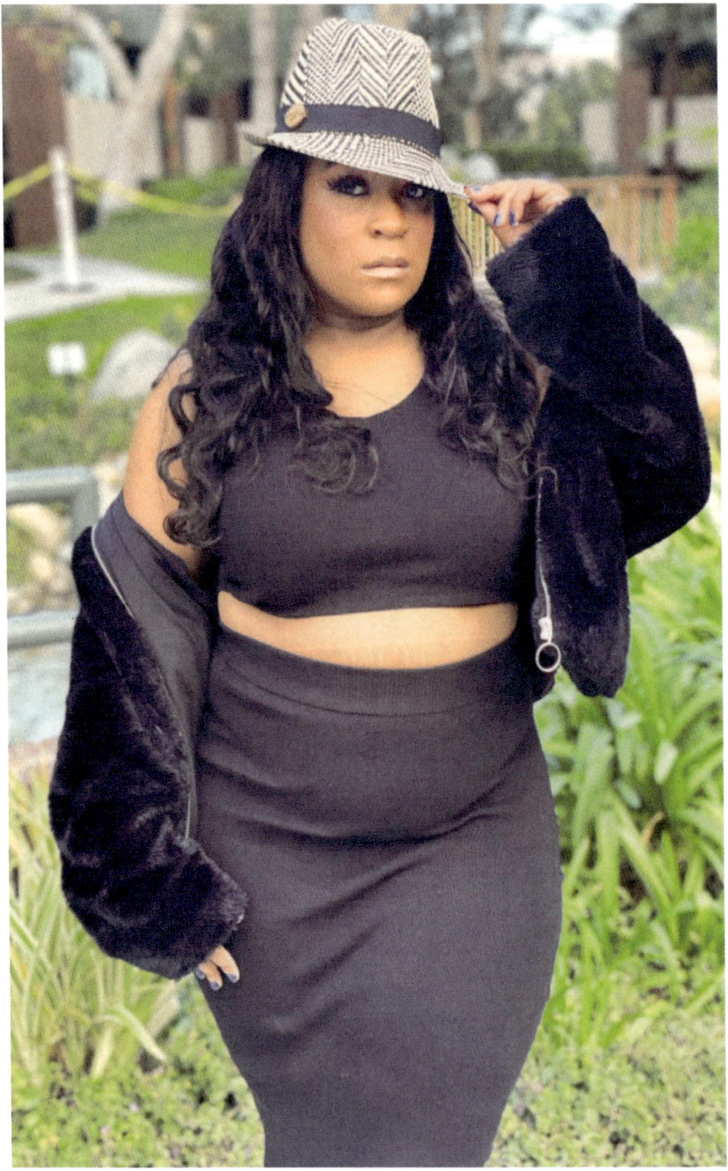

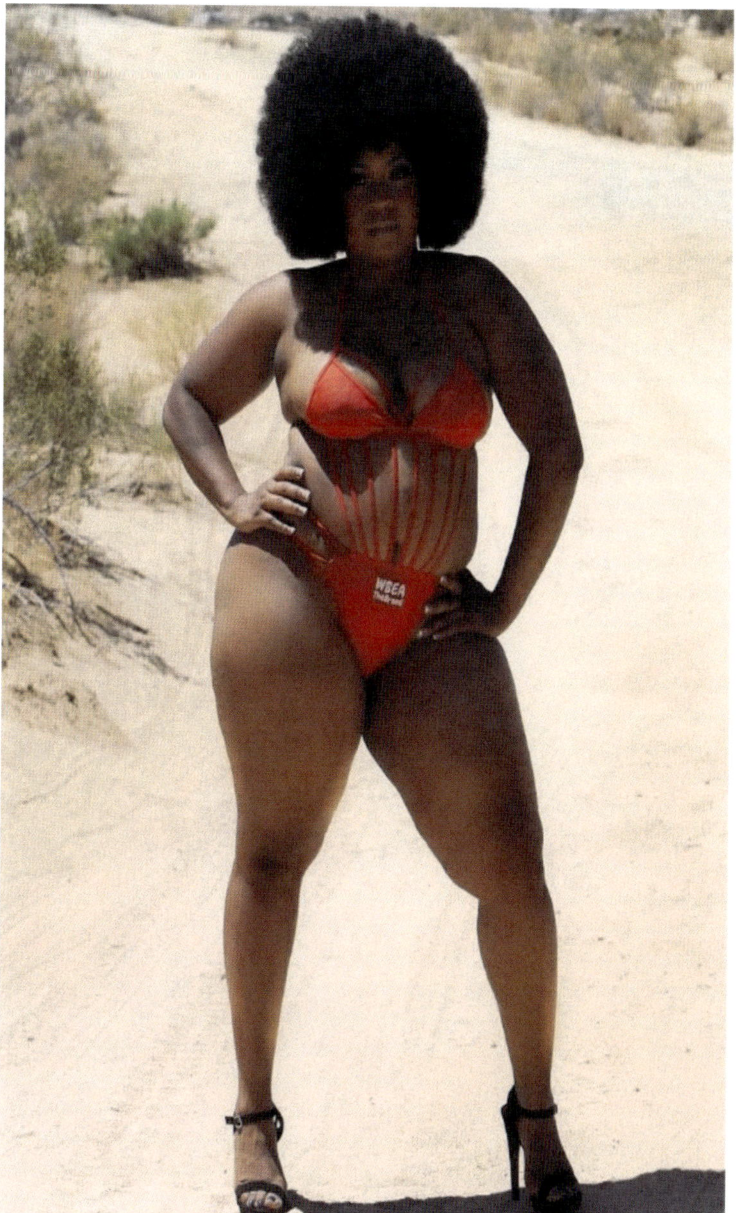

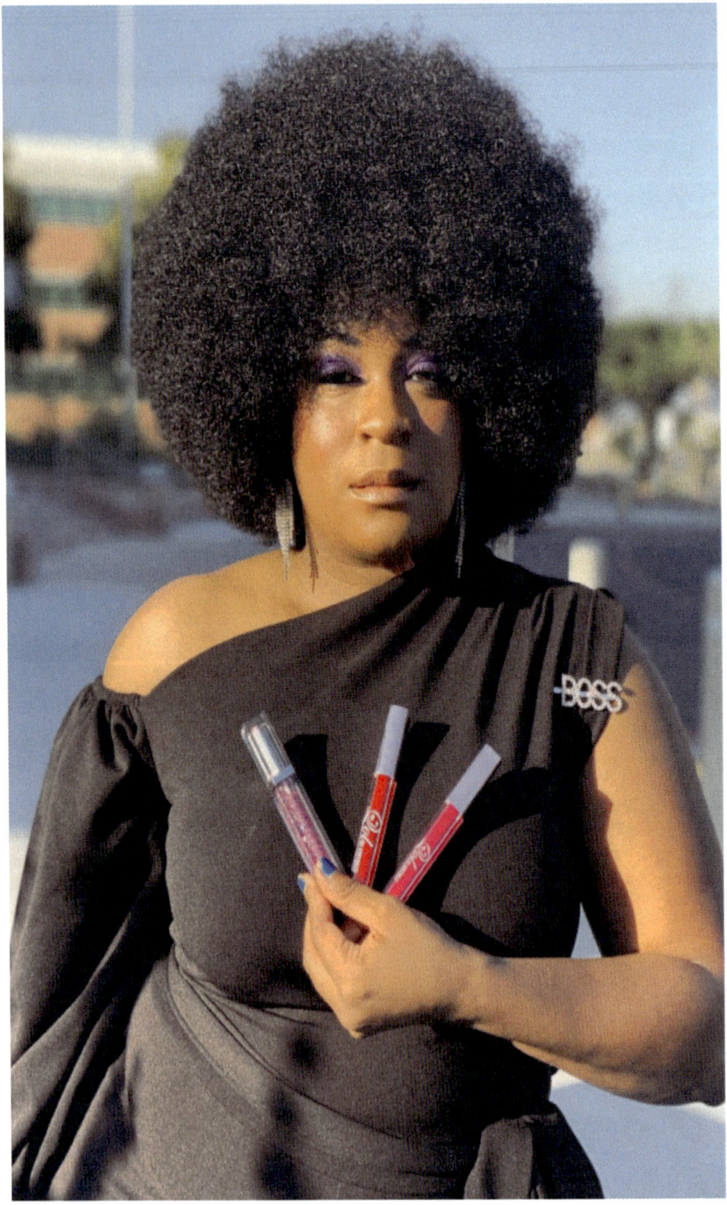
BOSS

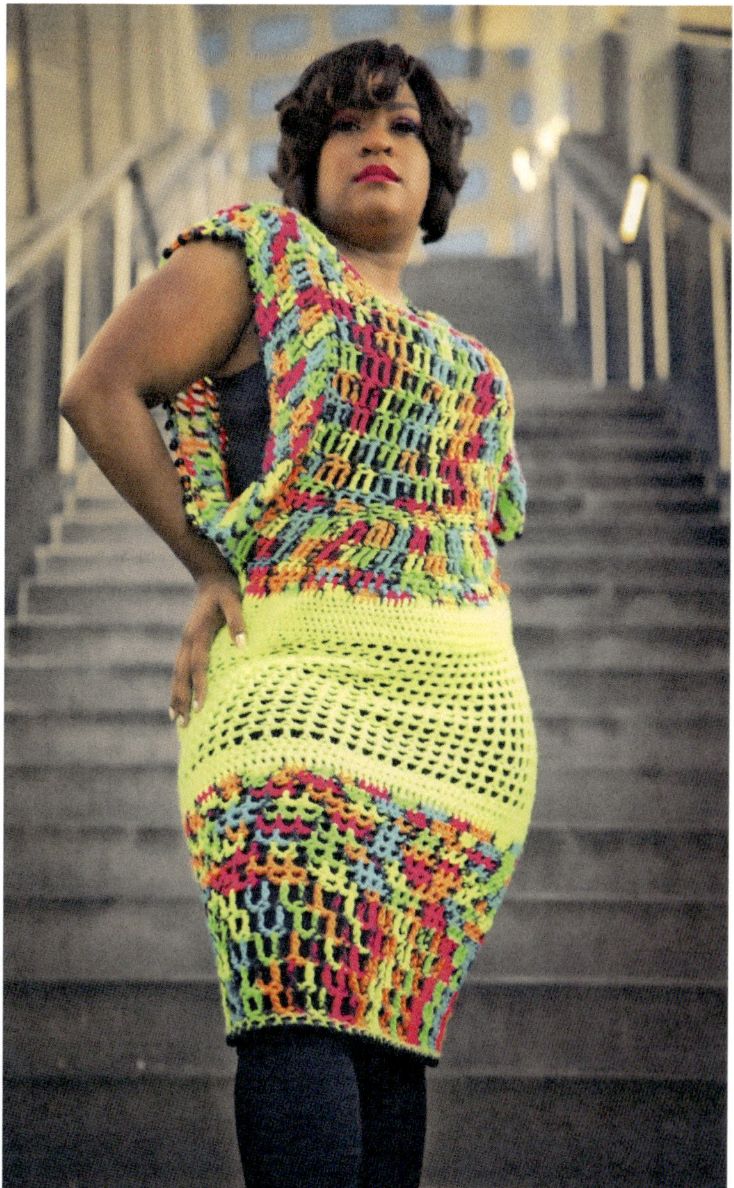

Made in the USA
Columbia, SC
04 August 2022